SEASCAPES

Ronald Jesty

HarperCollins*Publishers*

Special thanks to Leslie Seabrook for his valuable assistance
in the preparation of the copy for this book

First published in 1996 by
HarperCollins Publishers, London

**A catalogue record for this book is available
from the British Library**

Editor: Patsy North
Design Manager: Caroline Hill
Designer: Joan Curtis
Photographer: Jon Bouchier

ISBN 0 00 412784 6

Printed and bound by Rotolito Lombarda SpA, Milan, Italy

CONTENTS

Beached Boat, *watercolour, 18 × 34 cm (7 × 13½ in)*

PORTRAIT OF AN ARTIST

RONALD JESTY

▲ *Ronald Jesty at work in one of his favourite spots – Pulpit Rock, on the southernmost tip of Portland, Dorset.*

Ronald Jesty trained to be a draughtsman, then started a career as a graphic designer which lasted for over thirty years. In this capacity he produced designs and artwork for print, advertising and exhibitions. During his spare time he sketched and painted at every opportunity until, in 1978, he gave up his graphic design business in order to concentrate his attention on painting, especially in watercolours.

Living in Somerset, he has access to the nearby Dorset coast, an area which he particularly loves and where he finds many of his ideas and inspiration. Although the sea and

◀ Pulpit Rock 2
watercolour
28 × 20 cm (11 × 8 in)

coast provide the subjects which he most enjoys, Ronald also likes to paint still-lifes and landscapes. He believes that it is important to have sound working methods and basic disciplines when learning to paint. From this thorough grounding, a student's stylistic freedom and individuality can later emerge and develop.

Although he is a contributor to many publications on art and painting, this is the first book that he has written. He has been a part-time lecturer at his local College of Art and now teaches at an Art Centre.

In 1982 Ronald Jesty became a member of the Royal Society of British Artists. His work has also been included in many other national exhibitions, including the Royal Academy, the Royal Watercolour Society, Royal West of England Academy, Millfield Open Exhibition and the Singer and Friedlander/Sunday Times Watercolour Competition. In addition, he has held many successful one-man shows.

WHY PAINT SEASCAPES?

My childhood was spent in Weymouth, on the Dorset coast, within sight and smell of the sea. During the holidays, many happy hours were occupied on the seashore searching for hermit crabs, shells and pieces of driftwood, or exploring seaweed-covered rocks and pools for winkles, shrimps and anemones.

The harbour was always full of interest, with cargo ships and ferries from the Channel Islands, small pleasure craft and fishing boats constantly on the move. Elegant paddle-steamers took trippers along the coast to Lulworth Cove or Swanage, viewing the spectacular Purbeck cliffs en route.

In rough weather, it was an exciting experience to watch giant breakers crash on to Portland's cliffs, causing great showers of spray to burst into the air as we stood there, buffeted by the salt-laden wind. Staying until sunset gave the opportunity to see the lighthouse send its warning beam twenty miles into the darkness and an added thrill was to hear – and feel – the raucous blast of the fog-horn when mists swirled in from the sea.

Throughout history, ships of all sizes and kinds have been wrecked on treacherous cliffs, beaches and sand-banks and remind us of the sinister, cataclysmic power of the sea. Evidence of its force and action can be seen in the diverse geology of our coasts, where material is forever being eroded, washed away or deposited; cliffs crumble and fall whilst sand-banks, beaches and dunes shift and re-form to alter the shore's shape and character.

▲ Kimmeridge Ledges (*detail*) *watercolour*

WIDE VARIETY OF SUBJECTS

It is no wonder, then, that such diverse subjects provide the artist with continuous inspiration – from the sea itself in all its moods to beaches, rocks and cliffs, boats and shipping, seen under ever-changing skies which, themselves, provide many atmospheric compositions.

USING DIFFERENT MEDIA

A pencil is perhaps the simplest of all drawing materials and, although capable of highly finished and detailed work, is most commonly used as a medium for sketching, either to explore various aspects of subject matter or to collect and record information for later use. Similarly, pen and ink are often used in the same way but, whereas a pencil mark can be easily erased, pen lines are permanent and will require a more considered and disciplined approach. As a result, you may feel the need to gather a little confidence before committing yourself to pen and ink drawing for the first time, but after you have established a way of working with it you will soon enjoy its effectiveness.

▲ Lerryn
pencil
25 × 35 cm (10 × 14 in)
Perhaps the most commonly used sketching material, pencil is capable of a wide range of effects, whether in line or graduations of grey tones.

▼ Boat at Piraeus
fibre-tip pen
14 × 20.5 cm (5½ × 8 in)
I enjoyed the long, elegant shape of this boat, which I saw during a walk around the harbour. Making a drawing like this in a small sketchbook enables an artist to notice the details and shapes in a very concentrated and intense way – much more so than taking a casual look or a photograph would do.

▲ Cape Cod
pastel
23 × 34 cm (9 × 13½ in)
Midway between drawing and painting, pastels can be used in a combination of linear and broad colour effects. The colours are selected and drawn or rubbed directly on to the paper so that the desired result can be built up very quickly. However, the surface of the finished work can be rather fragile and should be protected.

▶ Cliff Huts, Portland
watercolour
33 × 23 cm (13 × 9 in)
This painting was made on the spot during one very hot morning when the paint dried quickly and the only sounds were of the gently lapping water and an occasional seabird. I worked fast as the tide was rising rapidly. Working in such conditions is sheer pleasure, even if the results do not always reach one's expectations!

Another medium which we tend to think of as a drawing process is pastel, since the sticks of this dry, chalk-like material are used to make linear marks or rubbed areas on tinted paper. At their best, pastels have a freshness of pure colour and an immediacy arising from the direct response with the paper. However, some artists find that mixing colours with this medium is less easy than with some others, and the pastels are also inclined to be somewhat dusty and powdery in use.

Watercolours and acrylics are ideal media for working out-of-doors since the equipment needed is, again, relatively simple and not difficult to carry. If there is a drawback with watercolour, it is that it sometimes takes a frustratingly long time to dry under humid or cold conditions. In addition, when once placed on to the paper, it is not easy to make alterations or adjustments, so that a certain amount of planning and decision-making is desirable. On the other hand, acrylic paints often actually dry more rapidly than one would like and this characteristic allows considerable overpainting without undue delay in either opaque or transparent colours.

The remaining important medium that you might like to consider is oil paint, which consists of pigments suspended in various oils, most commonly linseed. Since they dry relatively slowly, they have the advantage that they can be blended or manipulated on the support for some considerable time. However, when painting out-of-doors this can be a drawback for it will be apparent that handling and carrying wet, freshly painted boards or canvases, especially in a strong wind, may cause some difficulty! One big advantage of oil paint is that, as it dries, the colours remain true, unlike watercolours or acrylics which lighten and darken respectively to some degree.

A look at the examples included in this section will give an indication of some of the

◀ La Catelain, Guernsey
acrylic
18 × 25 cm (7 × 10 in)
This picture is quite small and was made, many weeks after we had returned home, from a sketch drawn on the spot but which also included some notes about the colours. Because of lack of time or rapidly changing conditions, this is a commonly used method of working and many of the examples reproduced in this book were made in this way.

subjects for which any of these media can be used, together with the kind of effects which can be achieved with them.

PATIENCE AND PERSEVERANCE

Drawing and painting are not always easy but success is more likely to come to those who persevere, so the first piece of advice might be in the form of encouragement to practise working regularly – half an hour's work each day will be much more useful than three hours once a week. The important thing is to enjoy looking at and experiencing a variety of seascapes, then painting the many exciting subjects that you will find in them as well as you can and with careful thought and planning.

But do not be disheartened if success does not come as quickly as you had hoped. Mistakes and failures happen to everyone and are the means by which an artist learns and makes steady progress.

▲ Mez Creis
oil
32 × 38 cm (12½ × 15 in)
Boats often make appealing pictures and the rich colours and surface textures of oil paint make it a good medium for such subjects.

MATERIALS AND EQUIPMENT

In a book of this sort it is not possible to give detailed advice about every product; therefore the following pages contain just a few suggestions with the beginner in mind. Start with a few simple, straightforward items, buying the best that you can afford, then add to them as and when the need arises.

WORKING OUTDOORS

Sitting in a wind from the sea can be a chilling experience so always be prepared with warm and/or waterproof clothing, also some tough shoes for walking over rocks or stony beaches. Being comfortable helps to make working out-of-doors enjoyable. Pack all your equipment into a rucksack or something similar so that at least one hand is free when negotiating steep paths and rocks.

DRAWING MATERIALS

Drawing papers are supplied conveniently as sketchbooks. A small size, such as A6, is unobtrusive in use but a larger size, say A3, will be needed for more serious work. Having spiral bindings to fold flat, the Daler-Rowney Series A is ideal for pencil or crayon work, whilst the smoother, harder paper of the Lyndhurst sketchbooks is also suitable for pen or wash drawing.

▲ *A selection of drawing materials and equipment. Some media, such as watercolour, can be combined, either in one or more colours, with pen and ink or crayons.*

Pencils are the most commonly used drawing tools, available in grades from 8H (hardest) to 8B (softest). Fairly soft pencils lend themselves to free sketching and HB (medium hardness), 2B and 4B are some that you should try. Don't forget a sharpener or a sharp penkife! Try not to rely on an eraser but, if you really must, have a soft putty one.

Pens are supplied in such an ever-growing assortment of different kinds that it is difficult to give more than general advice. Many artists require no more than a bottle of Indian ink and a penholder with a sketching nib, such as a Gillotte's 303. Others prefer a fountain pen filled with writing ink, whilst some use a 'reservoir' pen containing waterproof ink in a replaceable cartridge; the advantage of these is that they are always ready to use and, with them, work can be continued without interruption.

Some other drawing media which you should try are charcoal (twigs of charred wood), conté crayons, supplied in short square sticks of black, white and red-browns (soft and very responsive), coloured pencils, crayons and felt-tipped 'markers'.

WATERCOLOURS

Watercolour papers are supplied in three different surfaces: HP (hot pressed) is very smooth, Not (or cold pressed) has a medium texture and Rough, the most pronounced texture. The different surfaces affect the way the paint behaves on them and it is a good idea for you to try some of the different papers available. There are also various weights, resulting in different thicknesses. Papers known as 'Bockingford' and 'Waterford' in a medium weight of 300 gsm (140 lb) and a Not surface are recommended. These papers are supplied not only in sheets but also in blocks, which obviate the need for any preparation, such as 'stretching' (see page 14). Do not work on too small a size; 35×25 cm (14×10 in) should be a minimum.

Although more expensive initially, 'Artists' quality' watercolours have a greater intensity of colour and are more satisfying to use than the 'Students' quality'. I regularly use the following, from which almost any other colour can be made: Ultramarine Blue, Monestial Blue, Lemon Yellow, Cadmium Yellow, Raw Sienna, Burnt Sienna, Cadmium Red and Crimson Alizarin. Watercolour paint in tubes, being more fluid, is preferable when working at home, but pans of paint are more convenient out-of-doors.

Sable paintbrushes are a first choice, although they are extremely expensive. The more modestly priced Daler-Rowney's Series 34 round brushes in sizes 12, 8 and 4 are a good compromise, while their Series D77 brushes are even more economical and would be quite adequate. A large white palette with deep wells is desirable, but you could, instead, use a few white saucers. When working outside, use a folding watercolour box to take whole pans of colour; buy an empty box, then fill it with colours of your own choice.

You will also need a large water jar, a kitchen roll or other absorbent paper and, sooner or later, one or two boards of, say, 6 mm plywood about 40×50 cm (16×20 in) in size.

▼ *Some materials and equipment used in watercolour painting. It is worth experimenting with various papers and brushes to find out how they behave and how they suit your own personal style of work.*

PASTELS

These are powdered pigments made into sticks of (literally) hundreds of colours. Start with a small box of assorted colours before you buy any others you find that you need. Pastel drawing papers have a textured surface and are supplied in a range of tints. Those known as Ingres are available in two weights, either as sheets or, conveniently, as blocks or pads of assorted colours, thus providing a useful way to experiment with the different effects that can be obtained.

In order to prevent smudging, drawings of pastel, charcoal, conté and pencil should be sprayed with a fixative such as the colourless Perfix.

▲ *The box of 36 pastels makes an adequate selection to begin with. Fixative can be applied with the mouth spray shown or an aerosol.*

ACRYLICS

These are ideal for the beginner. The paints can be thinned with water or a special medium, overpainted as many times as you like and used on any non-greasy surface such as paper, card, hardboard, wood or canvas. Cryla brushes are specially designed for use with acrylics and you might try the Series C10 (round) in sizes 12, 8 and 5, for example, or the series C15 (flat).

Cryla paint is of a 'buttery' consistency but the Cryla Flow Formula is softer, more fluid and dries without brushmarks. To slow down the drying time of either by several hours, add some Gel Retarder. Suggested colours are as for watercolour painting plus a tube of Titanium White.

The only other requirements for using acrylics are a few rags and two jars of water – one for adding to paint, the other for washing out brushes.

▼ *Some of the materials and equipment required for acrylic painting. The rectangular 'Stay-wet' palette is designed to keep the colours moist during use.*

OILS

Daler or Canvas Boards are the most convenient painting supports for the beginner, being supplied ready-primed and in many sizes. Wood, watercolour paper or the smooth side of hardboard are excellent alternatives, but should be prepared with acrylic 'gesso' primer.

I prefer using a rectangular wood palette measuring about 40 × 30 cm (16 × 12 in), but cheap tear-off paper palettes could be used instead. Mix the colours on the palette with a knife. Hog bristle brushes in various shapes are used for oil painting. Illustrated here is a selection of round brushes suitable for detailed work; filberts, which provide a wide variety of marks; and flats, which carry a lot of paint for thick textural effects. I suggest that you try the filberts in sizes 8, 4 and 1 to begin with.

'Georgian' colours are suitable for your first oil paintings; get Lemon Yellow, Cadmium Yellow (hue), Cadmium Red (hue), Crimson Alizarin, French Ultramarine, Monestial Blue, Viridian (hue), Raw Sienna, Burnt Sienna, Burnt Umber and Titanium White.

Linseed oil and turpentine will also be needed; use them from a pair of 'dippers' clipped to your palette. Finally, have a few rags to hand ready for wiping brushes and so on.

USING EASELS

Folding lightweight easels are not usually suitable in windy conditions, nor stools on rough ground. However, when the occasion does arise, a Daler-Rowney aluminium Warwick easel, which weighs only 1.1 kg (2¼ lb) and folds into a neat package, would be a suitable choice. When working back at home and, especially for oils or acrylics, you may wish to consider buying a more robust easel. They vary from small table-top models, with limitations on stability and size, to the solidly built studio easels. So much depends on your available space and budget that it is advisable to compare different models at your local art shop before you decide.

▲ *A selection of oil painting materials. The larger palette knife is used for mixing paint on the palette; the smaller ones can be used for painting instead of brushes – the cranked shaft will keep the handle off the painted surface. The life of a brush will be extended considerably if it is cleaned thoroughly after use with white spirit, then soap and water.*

Tip

- When painting in oils, use a separate brush for each colour if you can, but until you have enough, clean any brush being used in white spirit and/or wipe it on a rag before picking up another colour.

PAINTING TECHNIQUES

This chapter summarizes the main principles of working with the various media. You will learn a great deal simply by trying them out for yourself and experimenting a little, but, if you feel that you need more 'in-depth' information, you may like to refer to the appropriate title in the *Learn to Paint* series.

WATERCOLOURS

The basic technique is in laying transparent 'washes' of colour which are allowed to dry undisturbed, any white shapes being left as untouched paper. Plan ahead to decide where such white (bare) paper or paler colours are to be reserved. Wash in the largest and/or lightest areas first before laying progressively stronger passages until, finally, you add the very darkest accents.

Paper in the form of a pad or a block is convenient to use, but working on the taut surface of stretched paper is a delight. To stretch it, cut lengths of 5 cm (2 in) wide gummed brown tape about 3 cm (1 in) longer than each side of the paper – do this first, whilst your fingers are still dry! Thoroughly wet the paper on both sides, then *very gently* blot off any surplus water. Lay it on a plywood board and secure it with the wetted tape, which is pressed down over each edge in turn. Let it dry naturally.

When mixing colours, first put a little more water than you think will be needed into a palette well. Then add paint with a brush to the required strength. Remember that as colour dries on the paper it will lighten slightly, but you will soon learn to allow for this.

▲ Cliffs at Studland (*detail*)
watercolour
The white cliffs are bare paper. A pale tint over the foreground was allowed to dry before painting in the dark colour around the leaf shapes.

LAYING A WASH
Raise the top of your board slightly and, with a fully loaded, large brush, run a band of colour across the top of the shape to be covered, then leave it undisturbed. Pick up more colour and lay another stroke in the opposite direction, below and just touching the first; the fluid paint will allow the two to merge. Continue in this way to the bottom. Colour can be varied by progressively diluting, strengthening or even changing it as you work downwards. The step-by-step demonstration on pages 44–45 shows this technique being used.

ACRYLICS

Acrylic colours dry very rapidly and, to keep them moist when working, it is worth having the specially designed Daler-Rowney Stay-wet palette. Alternatively, the addition of a little Gel Retarder will allow the paints to be worked for several hours. Keep your brushes wet during use as acrylics will quickly dry in them – permanently!

Any cartridge or watercolour papers can be used, taped or pinned to a board. However, card, wood or the smooth side of hardboard are more rigid supports and should be prepared with three coats of acrylic 'gesso' primer, the wood and hardboard being sanded first.

OPAQUE AND TRANSPARENT
Arrange your paints on the palette as shown on page 27 and use a palette knife when mixing them rather than brushes, which will soon become clogged.

Start work on the largest, most important areas by freely brushing on paint which has been thinned with water. The quick-drying advantages of acrylics are now apparent and you can soon overpaint with thicker, opaque colours to develop the work. Follow with any glazes – thin layers of transparent paint, enhanced by the addition of a little 'glazing medium' – which allow the underlying colours to glow through. Finally, any accents or highlights can be touched in with solid, opaque colours. The step-by-step demonstration shown on pages 62–63 will help to explain the process.

▲ Cliffs at Studland (*detail*)
acrylic
The colours here were laid one over another, some transparent, some opaque. Thicker paint was used for the white cliffs, then glazed over with weak, transparent tints in places.

Tip

- To make an alteration when using acrylics, paint over the incorrect area with a thick, creamy white; leave it to dry, then overpaint the new version.

The conveniently ready-primed and inexpensive Daler Boards are suitable supports on which to begin, but watercolour paper or the smooth side of hardboard prepared as for acrylics (see page 15) are other excellent surfaces. With a rag, rub some dull colour like Burnt Umber, well thinned with turpentine, over the white primer to give an intermediate tone to work from. Secure the board in an upright position on your easel. Arrange your colours on the palette as for acrylics, with turpentine and linseed oil in the separate dippers. Blend them as required with a palette knife, keeping your brushes for the painting itself.

THICK PAINT OVER THIN

There is no 'correct' way to paint in oils, but the following is a summary of the traditional method.

Using a large brush, freely scrub in the most important shapes with paints well thinned with turps, as a basis for the colours which follow. Then paint the darker areas, using less turpentine and allowing the work to dry at convenient stages to avoid brushing too much into wet paint. Deal, now, with the lighter, more opaque colours, gradually adding a little linseed oil, decreasing the turpentine and endeavouring, the whole time, to maintain correct tonal and colour relationships. The principle is to work from thin paint (with turps) to thicker paint (with less turps). Try to keep control, but if you lose your way in a confusion of wet paint, scrape it off with the palette knife, then start afresh after allowing a little time for drying.

▲ Cliffs at Studland (*detail*)
oil
Painting started by laying-in the dark areas of the sea, grasses and shadows using paint thinned with turpentine on watercolour paper primed with acrylic 'gesso'. More opaque, lighter, colours were then added and this 'close-up' illustration shows these, together with the textures of the brush marks in the final thick white paint.

Tip

- When painting with oils, use deliberate brushstrokes rather than a 'to and fro' movement (as in painting a door!), which would produce a smooth, textureless surface. Hold the brush well away from the ferrule and work at arm's length to give free movement.

▲ Cliffs at Studland (*detail*)
pastel
In this demonstration 'close-up', strokes of blue tints have been crosshatched with pale pink to produce the warm sky colours whilst yellow-green marks laid over blue provided the various tints of the sea. Notice how the green paper, left untouched in places, contributes its own colour and how it contrasts with the build-up of thick, solid white of the cliff.

Tip

● Pastels gradually become dirty with use. To clean them, gently shake the pieces in a bag with some ground rice, which is afterwards passed through a flour sieve.

Arrange your colours on a piece of corrugated card so that you can find each one easily.

Before making a drawing, experiment with different kinds of marks on scraps of paper, noting the effects of greater or less pressure, and of the use of the point, the sharp edges or the side of the stick. Mix your colours on the paper by 'crosshatching', but avoid too much blending of colours with your finger as this results in an unpleasantly smooth, slick effect.

DRAW AND FIX

Select a piece of Ingres paper, about 35 × 25 cm (14 × 10 in), in a mid-toned neutral tint appropriate to the subject. *Lightly* sketch the more important outlines in charcoal; then, using a mouth diffuser or an aerosol, spray on a light, even mist of fixative. This is to prevent the charcoal from dirtying the pastel colours which are to follow. Continue by establishing the main areas in pastel, the marks still being applied lightly. Fix again.

Heavier, more confident, freely drawn strokes can now be made and, at this stage, quite dense passages of colour can be produced by overdrawing a number of times and fixing. However, some artists prefer to leave the last marks unfixed in order to retain the freshness of those colours.

Protect the finished drawing with an overlay of tissue paper or by framing it behind glass as it can be damaged easily if rubbed or knocked.

DRAWING AND SKETCHING

▲ Fishermen's Sheds, Kimmeridge
Looking at the scene, you will find that a pair of L-shaped cards will help you to isolate the subject and decide on the picture shape. Adjust the positions of the cards and move them closer or farther away from your eye as you view the scene.

Drawing and sketching are a means of enquiry and discovery – a way of finding out what it really is that we are looking at. Making a drawing enables us to see things in a very acute and intense way, so that we are able to record our observations of all kinds in quite a special manner which could not have been achieved in any other way. Drawing can be used, also, as a method for considering problems of composition by seeing the subject resolved into a pattern of lines, shapes and tones on the flat surface of the paper.

Additionally, drawing and sketching are ways of finding and storing *ideas*. Even a simple, small sketch, taking no more than a few minutes to make, can be used and referred to at any time in the future. Yet, without it, the idea would quickly fade from our memory as other events take its place. Use your sketchbooks constantly and with any medium that suits your needs.

OBSERVING YOUR SUBJECT

Imagine, if you can, that we have walked down to the shore and come upon the scene shown in the photograph above left. Looking at it, the first impulse may be to draw everything in view, but it would be advisable to resist this temptation – for two main reasons. Firstly, there will be too much material to organize on your piece of paper; all the shapes will become very small and, consequently, difficult to draw well, so that the finished work will look weak and lacking in impact. Secondly, the sun, as it moves, will cause the light to change dramatically. Keeping the drawing simple will enable it to be completed within a reasonable time, before the conditions alter too much.

For your first sketches you will probably find that a 2B or 4B pencil and your A3 sketchbook of cartridge paper will be the easiest materials to use. If you are lucky you may find a spot where you can sit, either on a rock or a small folding stool. Make a start by looking at the subject and deciding where on your paper the main shapes will appear; then make a few tentative marks, either lines or dots, to indicate these positions. When making your first drawing marks, it is a good idea to leave enough surrounding space in case you find that you want to extend the drawing in one direction or another later. As you work, continually check what you have done to make sure that each part keeps to its correct proportion and position relative to the rest.

Almost certainly, and like everyone else, you will make an occasional mistake, but when this happens try to resist the use of an eraser to remove the offending mark. If you are tempted, it is quite likely that the replacement will be drawn in exactly the same place! Instead, use your first, misplaced, mark as a guide to the position of the correction. There is nothing wrong in leaving both marks as a part of your drawing.

Look for the quality of edges and outlines also. Some will be hard and strong, like those at the top of the roofs where they are seen against the bright sky; others will be weak and perhaps scarcely visible. Try to represent these differences by similar qualities in the lines you draw.

SKETCHES FOR REFERENCE

You may like your sketch to be a way of collecting information for use when making a painting back at home. If so, add written notes to the sketch about the colours, tones, light or anything else that might help you to recall the scene later. The usefulness of such notes depends on their accuracy and this will come with practice. The chapters in this book on Tone and Colour will give guidance on these aspects.

LOOKING FOR SUBJECTS

Whilst you are sketching and drawing, always be on the look-out for new subjects and ways of seeing them, seeking out some aspect which is unique or special. This may be in the shapes and patterns that you will find in natural objects – rocks and cliffs, plants, pebbles and sand, wave forms and reflections, clouds – or in man-made artefacts like boats, jetties and buildings, bollards, buoys, lobster pots or lighthouses. Other ideas may come from the strange and unusual colour combinations often seen near the coast, especially early or late in the day or in the winter.

▲ Fishermen's Sheds, Kimmeridge
pencil
A 4B pencil, as was used here, enables subtle gradations of tone to be employed. Keeping the shading lines in one direction gives cohesion and a uniform texture to the drawing. When you are sketching, leave out any details which you feel are unimportant, so that your drawing relies on a bold, strong structure.

◀ Cape Cornwall
pen and wash
30 × 42 cm (11¾ × 16½ in)
Broad washes of Sepia (brown) watercolour established the main tonal areas. These formed the basic structure of the drawing. Pen and ink lines then described the rock shapes, followed by written colour notes.

USING DIFFERENT MEDIA

After working with a pencil for a while, you may feel the need to experience other ways of recording what you see. I am fond of drawing with a pen, more often than not a fibre-tip or some kind of fountain pen; I like the clear definition of the black line on white paper, but I sometimes combine this with watercolour or crayon. Other media which you may like to try are the many different soft crayons, conté, charcoal or pastels which can be used in a much broader, even aggressive, way and are especially useful if you want to explore big, simplified shapes or to cover large areas quickly. Although some artists use these materials in a bold, free manner, others are able to use them with great precision and exploit their responsiveness to obtain great subtleties of line and tone.

Sketching need not be confined to linear methods of drawing and can be done, also, in any other medium, watercolours and acrylics particularly. Try

▼ Cliff House, Portland
pen and watercolour
42 × 30 cm (16½ × 11¾ in)
The colours were washed in first, quite freely, the pen lines being added afterwards. This sequence of working produces a livelier effect than merely filling in the outlines.

them all when you feel ready to do so; only then will you discover what they, and you, can achieve. At the same time, notice whether some methods suit particular subjects better than others.

Do not be too worried if your efforts do not always produce the results that you had hoped for – perhaps you feel that your drawing seems clumsy or inaccurate? If so, try to analyse your work to find out where it went wrong so that you may rectify the fault the next time and thus build on your mistakes. Be patient, for all artists have such experiences and have to practise continually to make progress.

◀ Rock Fissure
conté crayon
25 × 35 cm (10 × 14 in)
This sketch was made as a way of analysing the patterns of the rock structure and the water bursting through the rock fissure. Making any sketch will cause you to look at things with greater concentration and, consequently, acquire a better understanding of your subject.

▼ Trinity House Marker
watercolour
23 × 27 cm (9 × 10½ in)
In this sketch my interest was in the stark white obelisk against the blue sky, but the pattern made by the rocks was another important feature.

TONE

Relative lightnesses and darknesses are referred to as tonal values.They range, in nature, from the brightest light of the sun to the blackness of total shadow, but, in drawing and painting, only from white to black. The various tones of everything we see arise in two main ways. Firstly, the tonal values of an object itself are caused by the degree of lightness or darkness of its own colours and are referred to as 'local' tone. Secondly, light and shade produces its own tonal variations, depending on the quality and strength of light. Usually local tones and effects of light and shade are all seen together to a greater or lesser extent and it is always useful to be able to distinguish between them.

RECOGNIZING TONAL EFFECTS

The three illustrations of the harbour scene shown here will help to analyse and explain the different tonal effects. You can see from the larger picture how a combination of both local tone and light and shade are necessary to produce depth and realism in a scene such as this. Always try to define shapes by contrasts, however subtly, of dark against light and light against dark, allowing these tonal changes to do the work. It is not necessary to explain each and

a

b

c

▲ *The first illustration* **a** *is of local tones only – white walls, mid-tone roofs, dark trees, a band of colour around the lighthouse. Because the effect of light and shade has been disregarded, the result is a pattern of flat shapes. The second illustration* **b** *shows light and shade only (no local tones) and produces a strongly three-dimensional image. The subject is still recognizable even though some outlines have been lost, as at the base and left of the lighthouse and parts of the house on the right. Now if we combine the two effects in the same picture, the more realistic impression shown in illustration* **c** *appears and is what we usually expect to see.*

▲ Fort Doyle
watercolour
23 × 33 cm (9 × 13 in)
Strong sunshine from the side or in front gives the best opportunities to see the effects of light and shade. In clear air, unaffected by mist or cloud, the greatest tonal contrast here is between the bright sky and the silhouetted fort. You should also notice where some shadows are weakened by light reflected back into them from any surrounding bright surfaces, as seen here in the vertical sides of the rocks.

every edge with an outline; indeed, an edge which is missing here and there is more interesting to the viewer by allowing the contribution of his or her imagination in a small way.

From this, it will be seen that being able to judge and use tone well is one of the most important disciplines for any artist to acquire and it is worth spending some time in its study.

MEASURING TONE

One way of trying to assess tonal strengths is by 'squinting' at the subject through half-closed eyes. Another, more useful, way is in the form of the scale shown on the right and which you should make. This example was painted with acrylics on paper, but any other medium can be used.

Draw nine squares in a row, each about 4cm (1½ in) square, making one end white, the other a dense black. Now, using the black diluted with water if in watercolour, but mixed with white paint in other media, mix a grey which is midway in tonal strength between the white and black, making any adjustments to get it exactly right before you fill in the centre square (5) with it. Afterwards, fill the two middle spaces (3 and 7) with their respective light and dark greys before completing the scale.

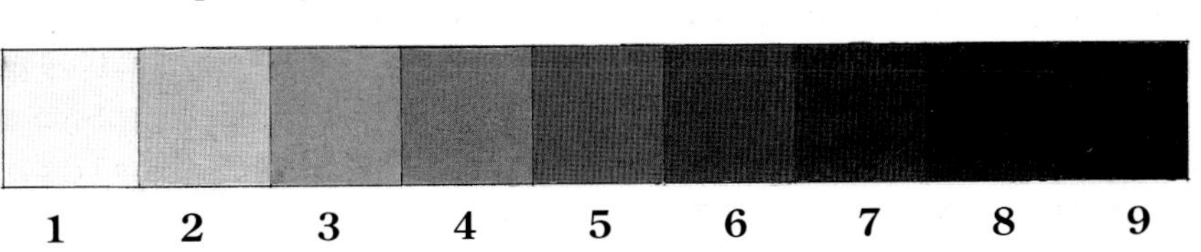

You should then have a smooth gradation of nine tones in even steps from white to black, but you may need to repeat the exercise several times before you achieve a perfect result. Use the scale to help you to compare the tonal values in the different passages of your subjects or painting.

Especially when time is short, tones from the scale can be recorded on outline sketches in the form of numbers, white being 1, through to black as 9. These can then be recalled and reinterpreted later in any work which you wish to make from the sketch. It is also a good exercise in itself, since you will have to depend on the accuracy of your own assessments of the tone strengths.

MOOD AND ATMOSPHERE

A painting which contains tones mainly from the light end of the scale is referred to as being in a 'high' key, from the dark end in a 'low' key. Each has its own effect on mood and colour, the low key tending to be serious, sombre or melancholic and the high key contributing to a more light-hearted and happy feeling. Nevertheless, a dark toned picture still needs one or two light areas in order to provide relief and contrast, vice versa for a light-toned picture.

Some seascapes, when seen on a dull, cloudy day will seem quite flat and uniform in tone yet, when strongly lit by sunshine, will suddenly become very contrasty under the effect of the

▼ Lone Fisherman
watercolour
23 × 32 cm (9 × 12½ in)
This picture depends on the shapes of the dark areas of tone contrasting with the pale surface of the rock. The quiet colours are of secondary importance. Notice that the fisherman's shoulders almost merge with the sea, but the sunlit head and white hair stand out from the darkness and help to explain the whole figure.

brilliant light and deep shadows. The atmosphere, particularly through haze and mist, has an effect on tonal values as well, in that things which might have had strong contrasts when seen nearby become paler and weakly contrasted when viewed at a greater distance.

TONAL STUDIES

You should now try making a series of drawings or paintings in a single colour such as black, Burnt Umber or Sepia. Use any of your sketches in which you have previously noted tone values by reference to the scale, as described on pages 23–24, or look for a simple subject which interests you out-of-doors.

Before you start work, decide how much depends on the effect of local tone values and how much influence comes from the effect of light and shade. Look, then, for the lightest and darkest points so that you can use them as a guide when evaluating the strengths of intermediate tones. Lastly, be aware of the overall balance of light and dark across the composition and whether the general tone might be in a high or a low key.

IN SUMMARY

Tonal control has important effects on every element of picture making – in contrasts of pattern, light and shade, depth, mood and colour.

▲ Rita Joyce
watercolour
30 × 42 cm (11¾ × 16½ in)
In an even light, without shadows, a mainly black-and-white subject such as this boat is ideal for a monochrome study of local tones. The extremes of light and dark will provide you with a guide by which to gauge the values of other tones between. Draw just one or two outlines lightly in pencil for guidance first, then make your painting with a single colour such as black or Sepia.

COLOUR

When starting to paint, you will soon be confronted with aspects of colour that may not have been apparent before and about which you will need to make decisions. Which particular colour do you see – grey, red, blue or whatever? What *kind* of blue? Greenish, or slightly violet perhaps? How bright or dull is it? How light or dark? One of the most important considerations is the judgement of tonal strength of a colour, since this will affect not only how light or how dark it is, but also how pure or intense. But there are other qualities of colours to be aware of and a colour wheel will help to explain some of them.

THE COLOUR WHEEL

This is a kind of map or diagram which shows colours laid out in a particular way. First of all, the three 'primary' colours **P** – red, yellow and blue – are seen in the centre. By mixing any pair of them in turn, green, violet and orange result; these are known as 'secondary' colours **S**. Further mixtures in the spaces between, like the yellow-green, yellow-orange, orange-red and so on, are referred to as 'intermediate' colours. You will see, also, that each colour has its own natural tone value, ranging from the lightest, yellow, through the reds on one side and blues on the other to violet, the darkest.

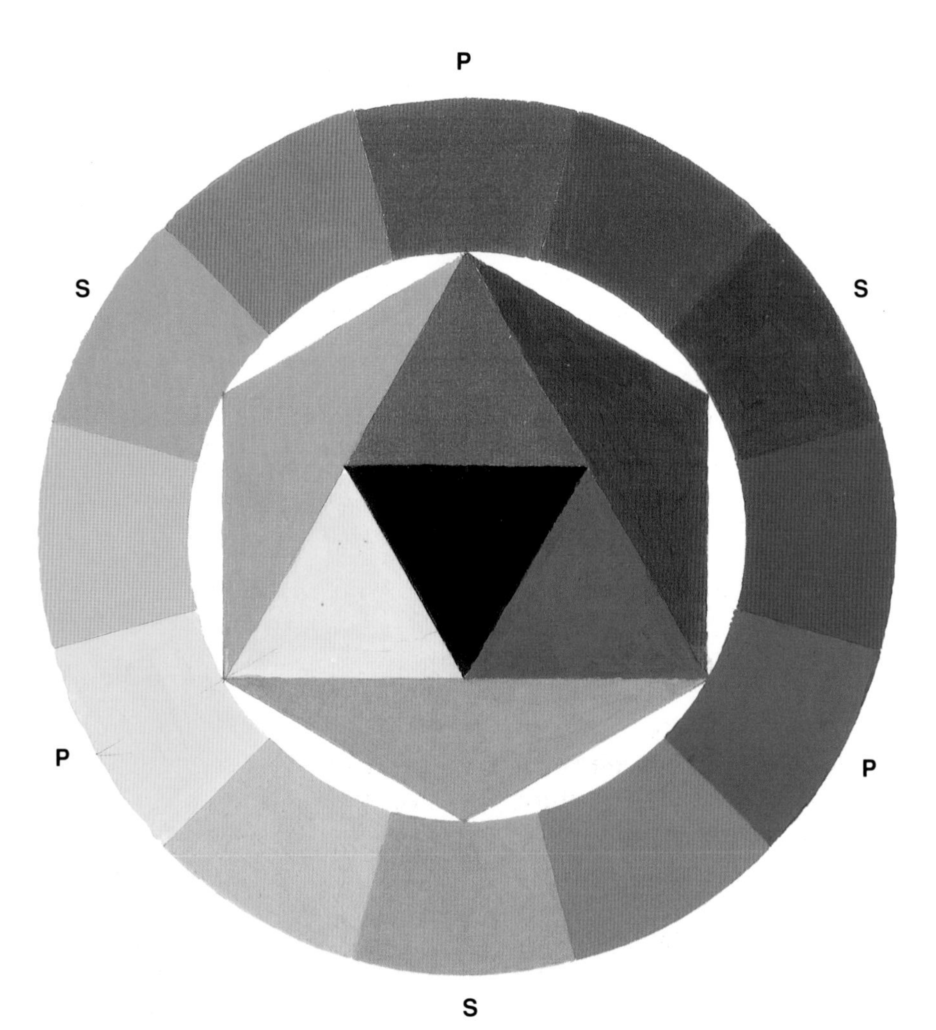

▲ *The colour wheel is made with the three 'primary' colours* **P**: *red, yellow and blue. The 'secondary'* **S** *and 'intermediate' colours are mixed from the following: Monestial Blue + Lemon Yellow = green group; Cadmium Yellow + Cadmium Red = orange group; Crimson Alizarin + Ultramarine = violet group. The black is mixed from red, yellow and blue.*

Incidentally, the red group of colours is described as being 'warm', the blue group 'cool', and each has its own particular effect in a picture.

COMPLEMENTARY COLOURS

Opposite pairs of colour which appear in the outer circle of the colour wheel, red and green, for instance, are known as 'complementaries' and are of

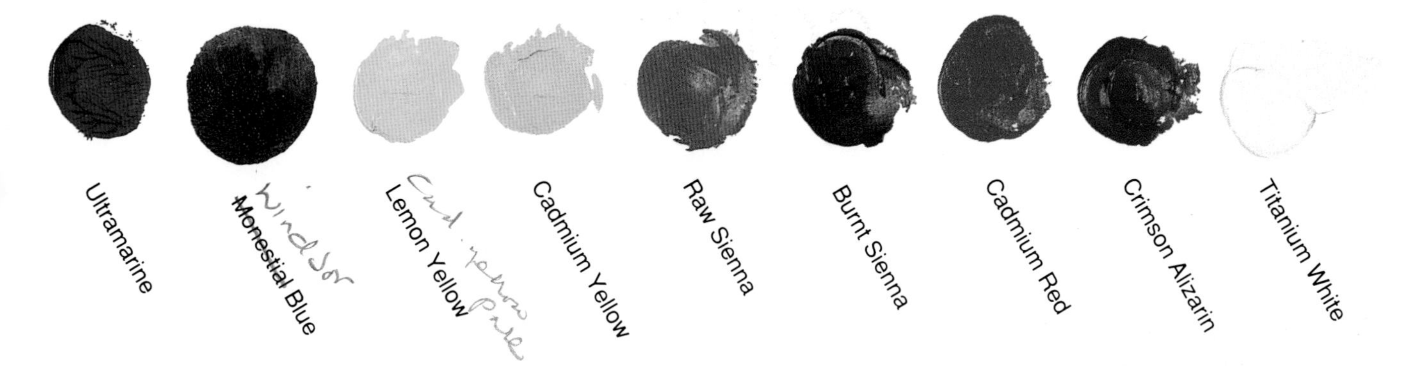

special interest to an artist. The reason is that, when either colour of such a pair is placed next to the other, they are both enhanced with a particular vibrancy yet, when mixed, they produce wide variations of greys, even black. This is worth remembering when making pictures since, by using complementaries, you can not only achieve more vivid colour effects, but also, conversely, make colours darker or duller (more grey) without the use of any black.

The colour wheel illustrates this in the central triangle of black, for it is, in fact, a mixture of the colours that make up the complementaries. In practice, by altering the balance of these colours, different 'blacks' are possible – bluish, greenish and so on. Then, when these are made lighter, many variations of grey can be produced.

COLOUR MIXING

If you have not already done so, you will, no doubt, be impatient to use your colours! Those listed on pages 11–13 are suggested basic selections from which you can mix almost any colour you want. Therefore, until you have gained some experience, you should not need to add any others. You will notice that no black or grey is included, for the reasons given above, although some experienced artists like to use them.

Try to get into the habit of laying out your paints always in the same order so that you will get to know where to find each one easily. I always arrange mine as shown in the diagram above, but you can choose any other sequence that suits you.

A good way to discover how various colour mixtures work is to make some simple charts like the examples overleaf. Do them in a methodical way on a fairly large piece of paper, working through a series using one colour mixed in turn with each of the other colours you have, followed by a second mixed with the other colours and so on. With dark colours like the blues, you may find it better to lighten them very slightly in order to see the colours more clearly.

Write down the colours used for each mixture and note the results, some of which may be surprising. For example, we normally expect blue and red to make violet, but Monestial Blue mixed with Cadmium Red will make a rather muddy grey instead of a good violet. However, do not disregard such an apparent failure as, at some point, you may need just this

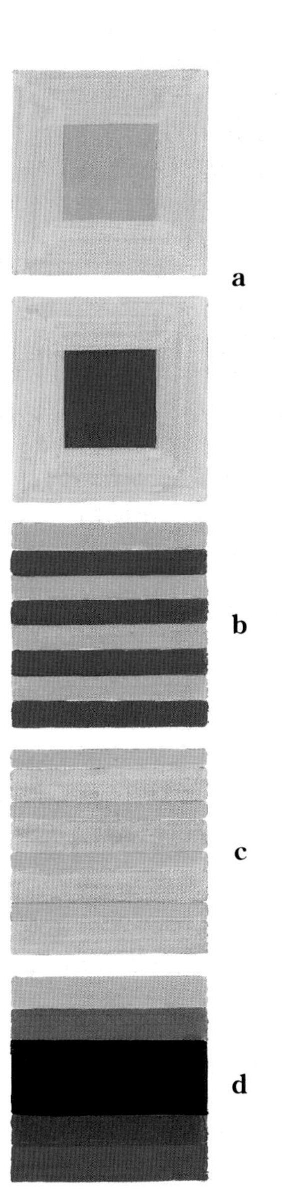

▲ *Complementary colours, blue and orange, shown separately* **a**, *then together as stripes* **b**. *Note the changed effect when the tones are the same* **c**. *When mixed, the two colours produce black or grey* **d**.

special kind of colour and it will be useful if you can remember how you made it. Ultramarine and Crimson Alizarin will mix to a much better violet, incidentally. In the same way, we assume that yellow and blue will make green and, although this is broadly true, it really depends on which blue and which yellow are used. Some examples have been included in the charts shown here to give indications as to what you can achieve in making greens and greys – colours which are often seen in seascapes. Other charts of colour mixtures which might be used for skies, rocks, beaches etc. are shown on pages 48 and 55.

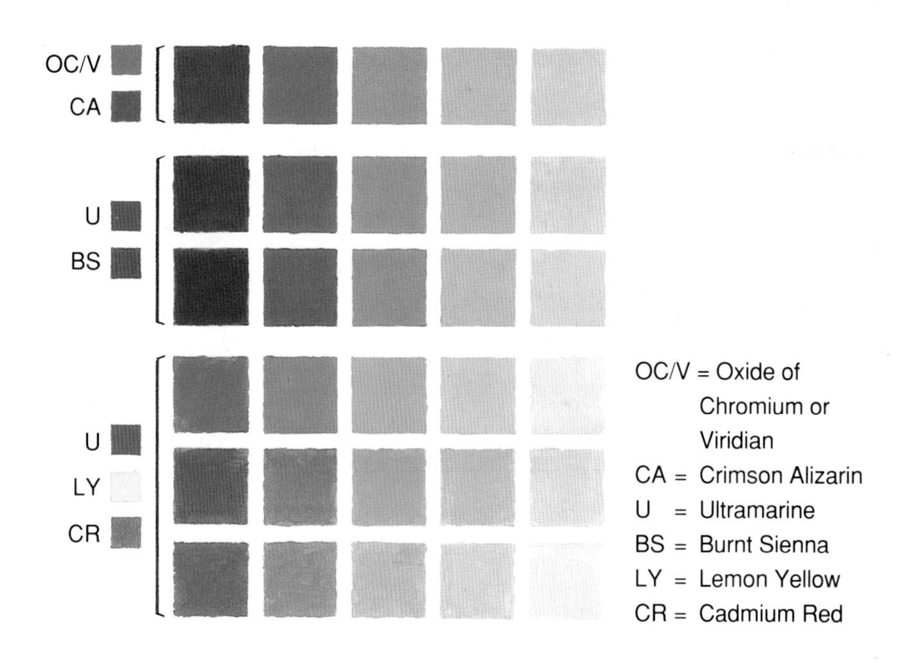

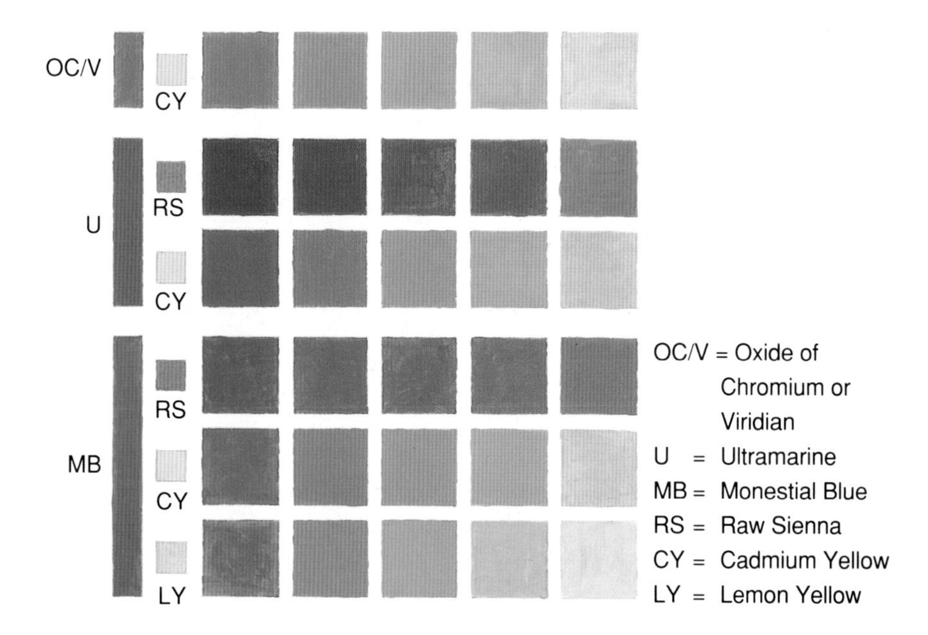

▲ *These charts suggest some ways of mixing the greens and greys that you might find in the sea. The range can be extended considerably and will provide most of what you need simply by altering the strengths and proportions of the colours. It is better to get to know thoroughly how a few such basic colours work, rather than 'collect' many which are unnecessary.*

Tips

- Cleaning brushes and palettes occasionally will help to keep your colours clean.
- When using watercolour, change the water frequently.

COLOUR AND TONE

In watercolours, tones are lightened by increasing the proportion of water to paint and thus the colour becomes weaker. Remember, always, to put out sufficient water first and *then* add colour to the correct strength. In acrylics or oils, white added to a colour lightens it but is also inclined to make it look 'chalky'. To avoid this, you can use a lighter colour of the same group instead, such as Lemon Yellow to lighten Raw Sienna.

If you are using pastels, avoid filling the paper texture with colours too soon, so that you can more satisfactorily lighten or modify your picture with overlaid strokes of other colours applied afterwards.

A colour can be darkened by adding its complementary, as with violet to darken yellow or blue-green with orange-red, and will be more interesting than if darkened with black or a grey.

A colour whose tone has been changed by making it lighter or darker will have its intensity, or brightness, reduced – the two are interlinked. Dull or muddy colours often arise from incorrect evaluation of tones, but it is easier to make colours look convincing if their tones are well-judged.

▲ Godrevy 5
watercolour
33 × 23 cm (13 × 9 in)
The colour in this painting is restricted to contrasts of warm and cool greys caused not only by the sombre rock colours, but also by the dominant effect of light and shade from the back lighting. Note that a strong focal point occurs at the greatest contrast of tone, where the bright light reflected off the sea is juxtaposed with the darkest rock shadows. The colours were mixed from Monestial Blue, French Ultramarine, Raw and Burnt Siennas and Crimson Alizarin.

A LIMITED PALETTE

For a little while, at least, it is a good idea to restrict and simplify the colours in your paintings to just three: a red, a yellow and a blue, such as Cadmium Red, Raw Sienna (used as yellow) and Monestial Blue. You will not be able to reproduce every colour exactly, but try to get as near as you possibly can. You will probably achieve more than you expected and discover a lot about colour mixing at the same time. Another colour combination might be Crimson Alizarin, Cadmium Yellow and Ultramarine. Compare the overall effect of this group with the first, then try some other variations of your own.

Always look for uncomplicated colour arrangements in your work – they will have much more impact than an uncontrolled riot of many colours. It is often a good idea to compose a picture from one group of colours, such as from a segment of the colour wheel, contrasting them with one or two bright accents of a complementary. Try contrasting 'greyed' or dulled hues with little areas of pure, bright versions of the same colours, or use arrangements of warm and cool colours. In such ways you will be less likely to finish up with a confusion of haphazard or unrelated colours.

It is also worth making some monochrome copies of your colour paintings, using only black or Burnt Umber (plus white for oils or acrylics) and being careful to match the tones of the colours exactly. Your tone scale will help you with this. Afterwards, look to see whether the copy has a good range of tones, neither too flat nor too 'jumpy', with unrelated dark or light accents. If you have a well-balanced arrangement of tonal contrasts, then it is likely that the colour painting will be satisfying also.

▲ Rock Pool 2
watercolour
50 × 50 cm (20 × 20 in)
Here, the inherent or underlying, though muted, hues of the rocks, known as 'local' colours, have been identified, then exaggerated by making them more pure and intense. In particular, the complementary red/greens and yellow/violets have been emphasized.

PERSPECTIVE

In painting seascapes and their associated subjects, you will almost certainly want to give an impression of depth and space in your pictures, perhaps to suggest the far distance of the cliffs or the way a boat on the beach looks solid and projects forward so that you feel that you can almost touch it, even though the surface on which it is drawn is flat. The aspect of drawing and painting which provides these effects is known as perspective.

It should be mentioned, however, that it is not absolutely essential to work in this way and, if you wish, you can make very satisfying pictures which are simply designs or patterns of shapes of flat colours that convey no indication of space or depth. Such a composition will tend to be decorative rather than realistic in its appearance.

OVERLAPPING SHAPES

This is by far the simplest way of suggesting depth and recession in a painting and is achieved by showing the shape of one object in front of, overlapping and partially obscuring another behind it which, in turn, is seen in front of another and so on. One can think of this idea being used to portray a succession of headlands receding into the distance, each partially overlapping the one behind, or of boats moored in a harbour, one

▲ Boats at Crinon
acrylic
27 × 18 cm (10½ × 7 in)

The boats are seen as shapes which overlap each other to give a feeling of recession and depth.

set in front of another. The number of suitable occasions when this kind of perspective can be employed is rather limited, however, but there are other methods of showing perspective which we can use instead of or as well as this.

LINEAR PERSPECTIVE

This method is the one we usually think of and is so-called from its use of lines to construct, measure proportions and describe solid objects on a flat surface, such as your sketchbook, to give an illusion of space, depth and differences of scale in a picture.

The basis of the system rests on an imaginary horizon known as the 'eye-level'; this is used as a reference line from which points and angles of other lines can be measured. The eye-level is placed at whatever height your eyes happen to be from ground level (whether you are kneeling, standing, or looking from the top of a cliff) and it stretches out horizontally to infinity.

A SINGLE VANISHING POINT

If we look at objects which are parallel to the observer's line of vision, any lines representing their horizontal edges, when extended forwards, will all converge and meet on the eye-level at one point, known as a 'vanishing point'. At the same time, an object appears smaller as it recedes into the distance, as explained by the illustration above right. Notice that lines from *below* the eye-level rise to meet it whereas those from *above* drop down to it.

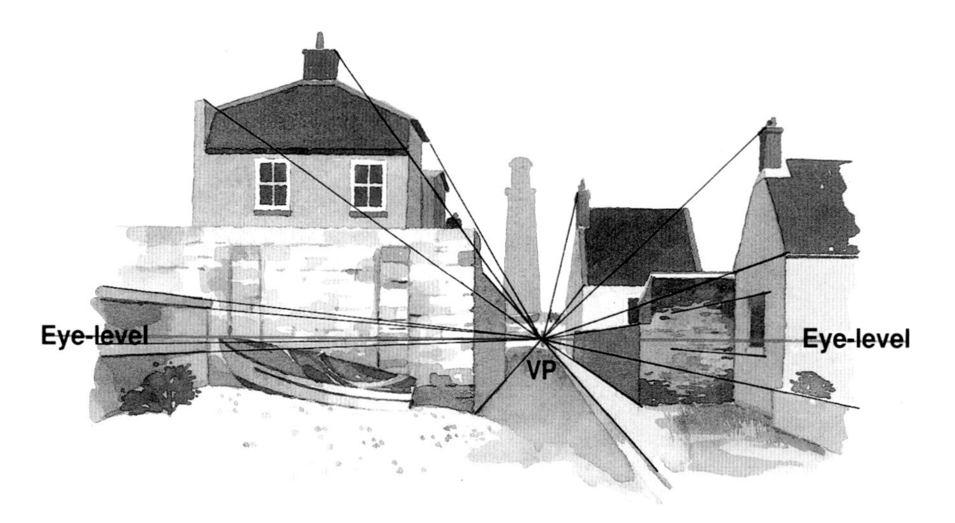

TWO VANISHING POINTS

If we look at an object from one of its corners, it will be apparent that there are now *two* sides visible which appear to diminish in size as they recede into the distance. Lines from the horizontal parallel edges, when extended, converge and meet at two vanishing points, one for each of the sides (see below).

▲ *The buildings here are seen frontally, from a 'square-on' viewpoint. Being parallel to each other, lines from their receding horizontal edges, when extended, all meet at one vanishing point,* **VP**.

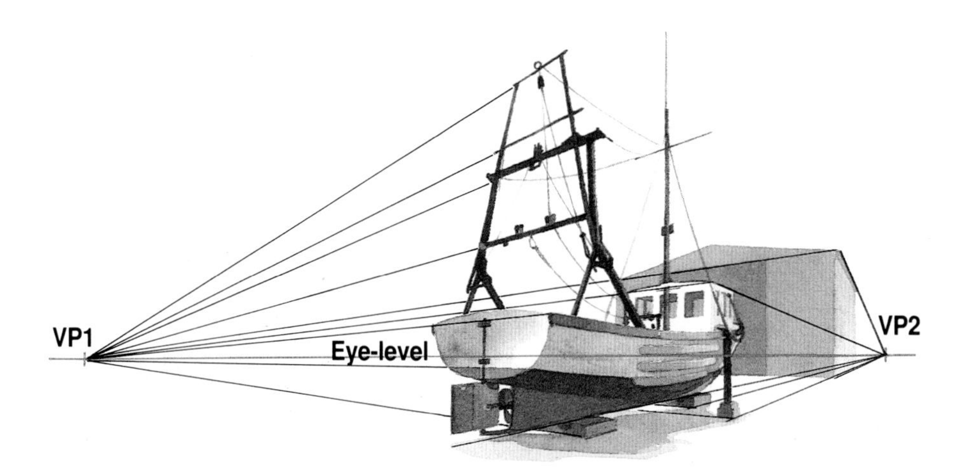

▲ *The boat in this illustration is seen from an oblique viewpoint. Lines from above the eye-level slope downwards to both left and right whilst those from below the eye-level slope upwards to meet at the two vanishing points,* **VP1** *and* **VP2**. *Here, the top of the rear of the cabin with its windows, the horizontal cross-beams of the fishing-gear and the stern, all being parallel to each other, can be seen to extend leftwards to meet at one of the two vanishing points,* **VP1**. *The side of the cabin, its windows, the bottom of the keel and the sides of the blocks on which the boat rests are all directed to the right, to converge at a second vanishing point,* **VP2**. *The same principle also applies to the boat-shed in the background.*

DIFFERENT VIEWPOINTS

If the artist now moves to a higher viewpoint to look down on a subject, the eye-level will, at the same time, move higher with him or her. Then, any lines extended from the subject below will slope upwards to their vanishing points on the eye-level. The opposite effect will occur for a subject seen from below.

Another circumstance occurs when objects are no longer lying parallel to each other but in various directions. Here, because some are turned to the left or right, their respective vanishing points will move to the left or right along the eye-level accordingly. The illustration (right) of boats lying below the quay wall shows an example of a high viewpoint and objects lying in different directions.

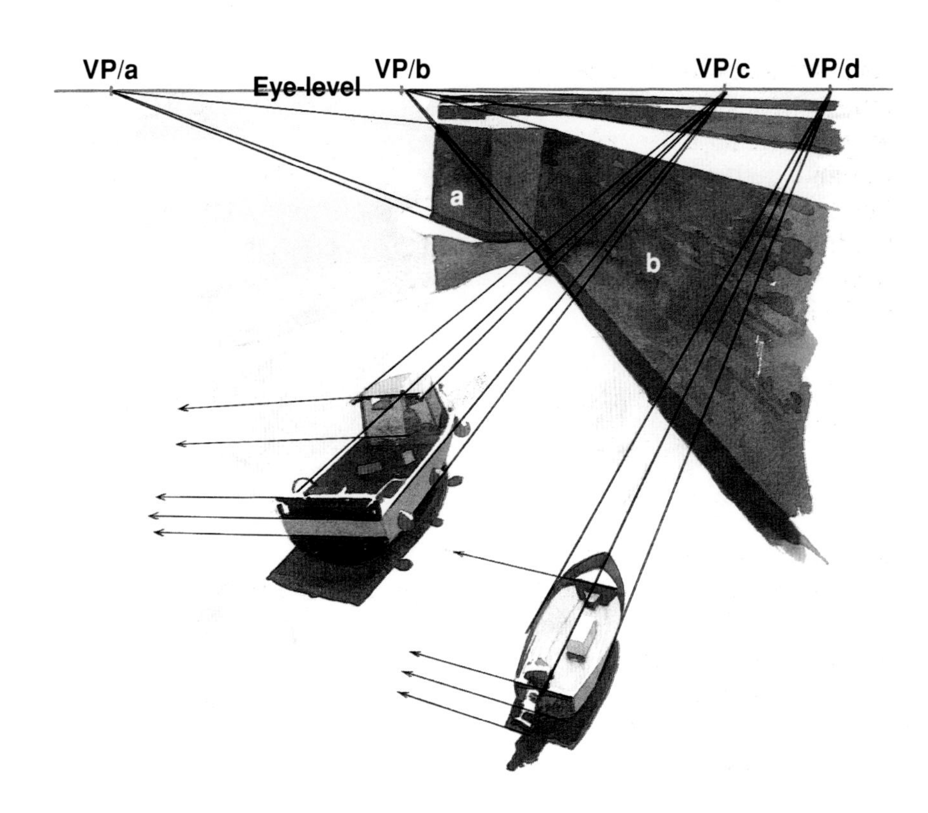

▲ *The eye-level here has been placed high within the picture area because of the downwards-looking viewpoint. The visible sides of the quay,* **a** *and* **b**, *are not parallel to each other and lines extended from their edges meet at separate vanishing points,* **VP/a** *and* **VP/b**, *on the eye-level. The two boats also lie in different directions and have their own vanishing points,* **VP/c** *and* **VP/d**. *Note that because the boat on the left is lying on its side, lines running across it from right to left are turned downwards at the left and will meet, not on the eye-level as usual, but at a point below it and some considerable distance outside the picture area to the left.*

MEASURING AND DRAWING

It is important to establish the position of the eye-level at the very beginning of your drawing since all else depends on it. Should it be at the top of the picture (high viewpoint) or low down (low viewpoint)? This is an over-simplification since you should also consider whether, in fact, you are looking upwards, even when at the top of a cliff or looking downwards when at sea level as this will affect what is to be included.

Use a pencil to make measurements. Firstly, holding it at arm's length in front of you, either horizontally or vertically, will enable you to judge the angles of any oblique lines. Secondly, and in a similar way, view the subject beyond so that, by sliding your thumb up or

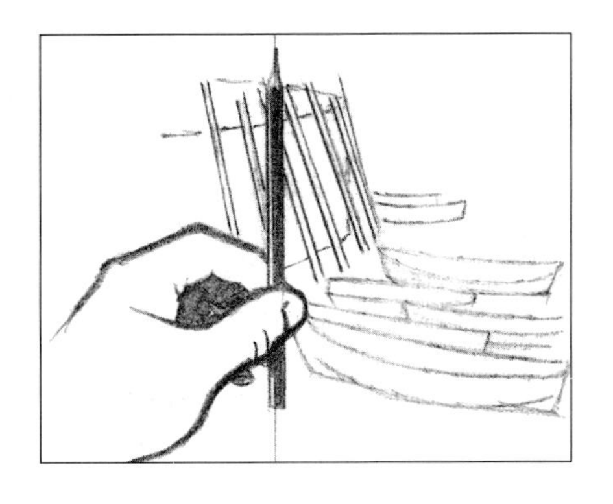

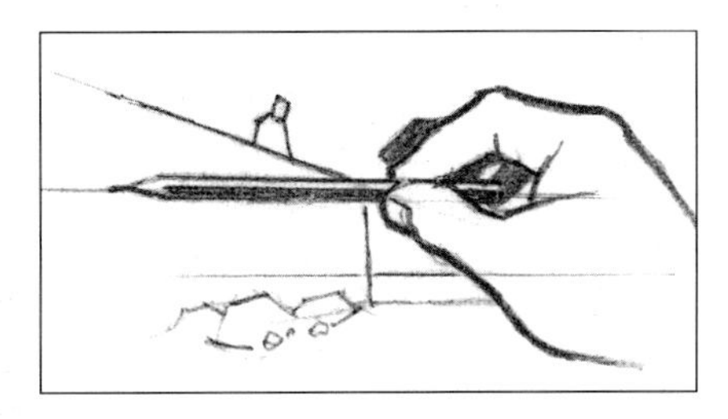

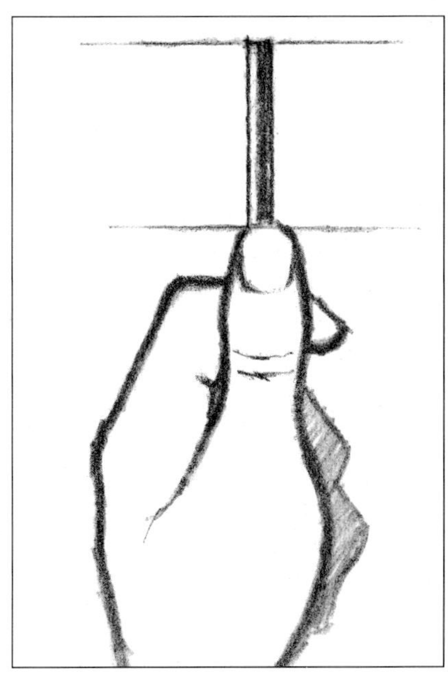

▲ *Using a pencil to measure angles and proportions.*

down the pencil, you may measure the length or width of some part. This measurement can then be used as a unit with which to gauge the relative proportions of other parts.

Construct the biggest, most important shapes first before adding the smaller details. Try not to rush your work, but spend time in checking your measurements and drawing.

AERIAL PERSPECTIVE

Sitting on a harbour wall we see the brilliant colours on nearby boats, their equipment and the buildings; all is sharply defined and contrasted in terms of local colour, tone, light and shade. Yet, looking into the distance along the coast, similar boats are much less bright, their colours muted, outlines less definite. The cliffs have a pale violet-grey appearance although we know that, if seen closely, they are a warm, sandy colour. This is 'aerial perspective', the result of atmospheric haze which always seems to be present to some degree, even on the clearest day.

Use this effect as another way of bringing the idea of space and distance into your paintings. Reserve the greatest contrasts of colour, tone and definition for whatever is nearest, then look to see how the farther areas become more dull, blue, violet or grey, more weakly contrasted and softly edged as they recede into the haze of the distance.

LIGHT AND SHADE

Finally, do not forget the use of light and shade as another way to give an illusion of depth.

▼ Loch Linnhe from Port Appin
watercolour
30.5 × 51 cm (12 × 20 in)
Aerial perspective, overlaps and diminishing scale are used to give a sense of depth and space. Notice that not only are the hills weaker and greyer as they recede, but so are the clouds in a similar way. The rocks in the foreground of the picture seem close by virtue of their detail, contrasts of tone and colour.

COMPOSITION

It cannot be stressed too strongly that the most important consideration in any drawing or painting lies in its composition. This means the orderly arrangement, or design, of the shapes of different colours and tones in a way that will express your ideas and intentions clearly. A painting can be brilliantly executed technically, yet fail in its purpose if its component parts are presented in a confusing or haphazard manner.

Each one of us has his or her own individual outlook, interests and experiences which affect our thoughts and degrees of imagination. It will be your own unique combination of ideas, preferences and decisions that will enable you, through the compositions in your work, to express your feelings about your choice of subject matter in a very personal and creative way.

ISOLATING THE SUBJECT

Suitable images and ideas for your compositions are usually closer than you think. How often have we wasted time in travelling many miles in search of painting subjects only to find them on our own doorstep upon our return! Therefore, look first within the immediate surroundings of whatever seashore or harbour you happen to be visiting. Use the L-shaped cards, already described on page 18, to help you to isolate your subject matter from the mass of detail which surrounds it by varying the proportions of the viewing rectangle, moving it nearer or farther from your eye or turning it vertically if the subject suggests it.

Look at the scene before you and endeavour to see it as an arrangement of flat shapes and, in this way, consider the possibilities for a composition on your flat piece of paper, board or canvas. It will then be easier to build on this simplified idea and to develop a feeling of depth and space afterwards.

▲ Boats at Kimmeridge
watercolour
16 × 24 cm (6¼ × 9½ in)
This composition is mainly concerned with patterns but, to a lesser degree, with the effect of light and shade also. Horizontal shapes of the boats, lengths of wood and the landscape behind, all in cool colours, contrast with the warmly tinted rock shapes below. The white boat is focused by the strongly contrasted tones, especially at the point where the sky meets it.

▲ *These are two versions of the same scene and show how emphasis can be focused on to one particular area and/or the mood changed by manipulating the tonal arrangement – light against dark, dark against light. Colours and proportions can be varied for similar reasons. Making small sketches like these will enable you to consider and choose one idea in preference to another before committing yourself to a more finished work.*

TAKING A BROAD VIEW

Even at this early stage you must try to discover the essence of the subject, its uniqueness, and begin to choose and select. At first, deciding what is important and what is not will be difficult, but an ability to recognize the big shapes and broad areas of tone and colour will be advantageous. Such large masses are invaluable in providing a strong structural basis to any composition. Once again, try to disregard all irrelevant detail.

In attempting to reach your decisions, it will be helpful to make many preliminary small thumbnail tonal sketches with a soft pencil, charcoal or something similar. In this way you will be able see what your ideas look like as simple shapes of different tones on a flat surface using just one or two greys, a black and the white of the paper.

PAINT QUALITIES, NOT THINGS

Many compositional ideas may be found in interesting and beautiful patterns of colour, of harmonious and related hues or of sometimes surprising contrasts – a small spot of bright pure colour against a larger area of some dull shade perhaps, or complementaries, or variations of warm and cool colours. Other colour schemes may come from quiet neutrals in varied tones, whether of the reflections seen in murky waters, rocks of diverse geological origins or the tints of grey skies and mists.

You will always find an infinite variety of patterns and shapes near the sea which provide many a subject to paint – rock and cliff formations, pebbles and beaches, wave forms, man-made structures like sea-walls and quays, boats, masts and nets; in addition, the textures of gritty rock and concrete surfaces contrast with sea-washed wood, rusty iron rings and chains, plastic buoys and light reflected off still water.

Such qualities of pattern and texture, colour, tone and line are the true building blocks of any composition and are more important than the very objects that produce them. Learning how they can work together in a cohesive, balanced composition is an exciting process with endless possibilities.

▲ Godrevy Lighthouse
watercolour
12 × 40 cm (4¾ × 15¾ in)
The long picture shape here reflects the wide vista of the subject matter. Compositionally, the horizon is just above the centre line to allow a greater space below, whilst the rhythm of cloud shapes gives movement across the sky in what might otherwise be a static composition. The horizontal theme is interrupted by the vertical shape of the lighthouse and its reflection, thus providing a focal point in the picture.

PICTURE ORGANIZATION

Your chosen subject matter will, to some extent, dictate the picture size and shape and whether the format should be horizontal or vertical. The medium you choose and the practical considerations of the way you work will also have a bearing on the size of any painting. Generally speaking, seascapes suggest wide, horizontal vistas of a peaceful and serene character, whereas a vertical format can be dramatic and confrontational, as in the idea of cliffs or tall structures. Square pictures are less easy to organize because each side is of equal length and thus there is a certain ambiguity.

Dividing a blank picture area into the proportions of its main shapes and spaces may seem problematical, but the following simple guidelines will help.

Start with a clear idea of the purpose of the composition and what it is about your chosen subject that you wish to portray. Make some decisions about the order and importance of each component so that your 'message' will be expressed clearly, then arrange the lesser priorities of other picture qualities.

Choose the position of your viewpoint and eye-level, as these will not only affect the placing of the first horizontal division of space but will also determine the character of the picture. For example, a high viewpoint will display a widely spaced area, remote and isolated from the onlooker; a normal eye-level shows the scene as we usually see it and so may not be especially exciting, whilst a low viewpoint can be dramatic and strange, even somewhat threatening if we are close to the subject.

THE FOCAL POINT

Every composition should have an area of special interest – a focal point – to which the eye will be led by way of other, lesser, points of interest. The focal point often carries the greatest contrasts of tone and/or colour and, in this way, draws our attention. This area of special interest and importance should be positioned with some care so that the picture area is divided in a well-balanced but not a symmetrical way.

Always avoid an equal balance of proportion or weight as the

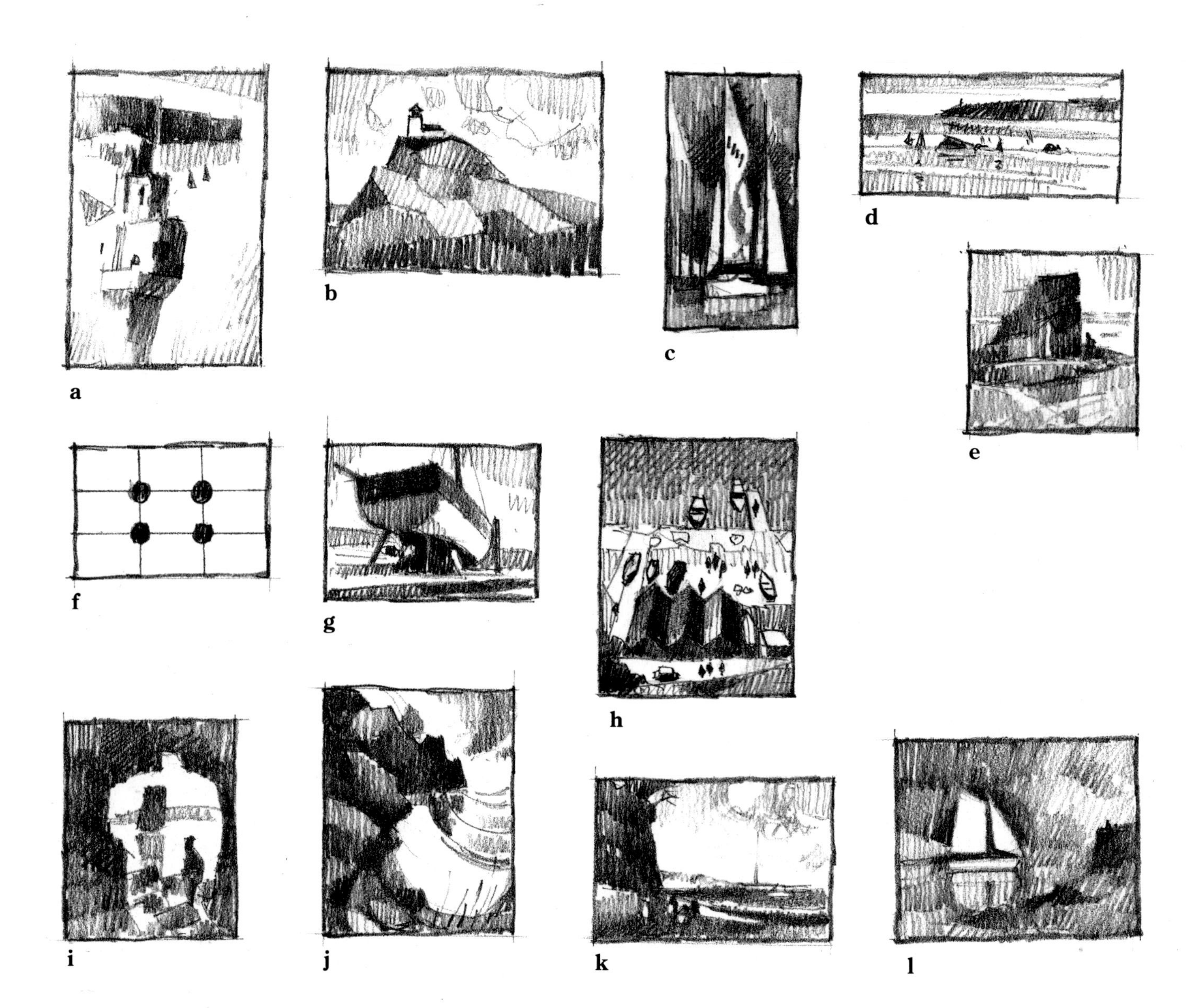

effect is certain to be boring and will have the disadvantage of an equal division of interest. This will occur, for instance, if the horizon is placed halfway down the picture. A simple rule is to imagine the picture area divided into thirds, both vertically and horizontally, and to use the intersection of any of the dividing lines on which to position your main focal point. In this way you will also avoid using weak areas such as the centre or edges of the picture.

Your design will have greater strength and stability if the main subject areas are resting on a solid base of one or two big shapes – a sort of platform – placed across the foot of the composition. Without some construction of this sort, there is a possibility that the design will look uneasy or even give the impression that something is about to fall through the bottom of the picture!

As discussed earlier, the tonal pitch will have a bearing on the mood and atmosphere – a low key of predominantly darker tones will induce a solemn or serious mood, whilst a high key will suggest something more light-hearted and cheerful.

▲ *Some thoughts on composition*
a *Instability*
b *Stability*
c,d,e *Picture formats suggested by disposition of subject*
f *Division by thirds: bold dots indicate suitable positions around which to place a focal point – avoid the centre and edges*

A few compositional suggestions
g *Low viewpoint*
h *High viewpoint*
i *O-shaped layout*
j *Spiral layout*
k *L-shaped layout*
l *Contrast of tone: light against dark, dark against light*

You may feel that making formal arrangements of all these components – the colour scheme, contrasts of light and dark, the balance of small and large shapes and patterns, the effects of scale, perspective and so on – may seem contrived. Although they are necessary, try not to let such thoughts stifle your natural instincts and feelings too much, especially when you come across things that look strange or do not conform to preconceived ideas. But be conscious of the rules and rely on them to provide some sense of order in every picture you make.

Finally, try to find the opportunity to study the work of such famous seascape artists as J. M. W. Turner, Eugène Boudin and Winslow Homer. Discover the ways in which they designed and composed their masterpieces, perhaps by translating some of them for your own subject matter.

▲ Old Harry Rocks
watercolour
48 × 30.5 cm (19 × 12 in)
This composition is deliberately unstable and looks uneasy as a way to emphasize the feeling of vertigo in looking down from a high point. The white cliff face seemingly hangs in space, but there is also a feeling of insecurity and of falling down into the emptiness at the foot of the picture. The normal compositional rules have been broken in order to create a particular effect.

Tip

- Keep your compositions simple. A few bold shapes of well-judged tones and colours in the right places will have a much greater impact than a picture which is filled with a confusion of irrelevant detail.

THE SEA

The element which is common to almost every seascape is, of course, the sea itself. Between the extremes of quiet, limpid waters in some secluded harbour and the violence of great ocean breakers crashing on to a vertical cliff face, the sea is never devoid of interest or some visual exhilaration. It is, to some extent, always moving and changing under the effects of the weather and light, the ebb and flow of the tides and its contact with the coast.

When drawing and painting the sea, it is important to realize that, although liquid and fairly transparent, it is still subject to the usual disciplines such as pattern, tone, colour and perspective.

REFLECTIONS

Perhaps the best starting point is not with the open sea but in a sheltered corner where the water is comparatively still, the weather quiet and conditions not likely to change quickly. Here, reflections are likely to be a feature, but they can be confusing if you are studying them for the first time.

The colours of objects, when reflected, become modified in that they lose their intensity, or brightness, the extent depending on the suffusion of any colour or muddiness from the water itself. Similarly, tonal values are altered by the fact that light tones become less light and dark tones less dark. Sometimes, and surprisingly, the reflected tone from an object becomes altered completely; for example, a white post standing in water may have a dark reflection.

You will notice that reflections occur when you look *across* the water surface more or less horizontally but, if you lower your eyes, you will begin to see the sand and pebbles of the nearby sea-bed *through* the water below. At a midway point, weak reflections can still be seen but are superimposed on your image of the sea-bed. This is one phenomenon in particular which you will have to consider carefully if you decide to paint it. Indeed, because some of the effects seen in or on water are often quite unpredictable, it is not good practice to guess at them but to rely only on your own observations and discoveries.

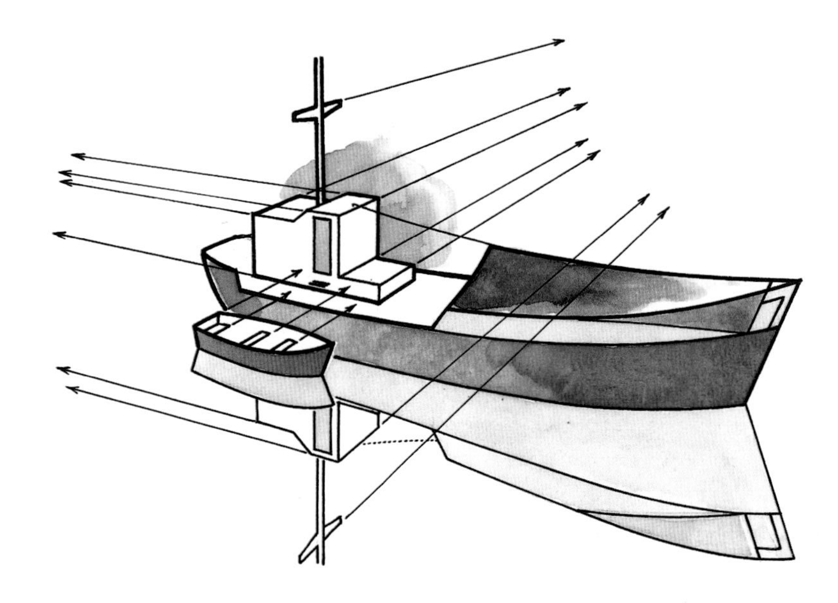

▲ *Imagine this reflection as an inverted image of the two boats – it may help if you turn the page upside-down. Lines from both the boats and the reflection will extend to common vanishing points.*

▲ Cloud Reflections
acrylic
20 × 25 cm (8 × 10 in)
The sea nearly always has a certain amount of movement, so this rare occasion of absolute stillness offers the unusual sight of perfect reflections in the water.

◀ Rough Sea
watercolour
21 × 30 cm (8¼ × 11¾ in)
The sea is often extremely agitated and confused, but making a sketch will cause you to spend time in looking and identifying the kinds of simplified marks, colours and tones you will need. Notice that the tone of the sea here is resolved into just one or two green-greys with patches of white foam. The accidental paint splashes are indications of the buffeting wind, which threatened to blow everything away!

ROUGH SEAS

Even on a rough sea, reflections of big shapes and colours from the sky can be detected, though diffused and weakened by the myriad of agitated and swirling facets of the water's surface. The effect is enough, nevertheless, to influence the colours of the sea in such a way that there is always a harmony between it and the sky.

Under the effects of strong winds, the sea is at its most exciting but, at the same time, produces the most difficult conditions for drawing and sketching. Because of the ceaseless movement, it is essential to spend time just observing and trying to understand what is happening before you. Notice how the shapes and arrangements of the nearby waves change as they meet the obstacles of the shore – whether a shelving beach, submerged or exposed rocks, or perhaps a quay or pier. What is the pattern of movement when the water hits these obstacles, then slides around and over them

▲ Breakers, Godrevy
watercolour
25 × 25 cm (10 × 10 in)
This sketch is no more than an impression of the action of a rough sea. To simplify painting of this kind, it helps to reduce the number of colours used – Monestial and Ultramarine Blues, both Siennas and Crimson Alizarin in this case.

before subsiding, only to be sucked under the next approaching mass of water? How often does a particular sequence repeat itself – and, then, how soon will it appear before you once more? Which part of the movement is it that interests you most and that you would like to use as a subject?

To help you to make up your mind, draw some simple sketches, mere diagrams, of whatever it is that interests you, repeating them as many times as necessary until you feel confident about how much to include and the effect that you want.

COLOURS OF THE SEA

As with reflections and movement, the best way to get to know the colours of the sea will only be by your own observations and study. There is no formula to say that you should use either this or that colour or mixture. So much depends on the conditions, such as the influence and effect of the clouds and sky, the strength and position of the light or how agitated and wind-blown the surface might be.

In times of bad weather, shallow water near the shore takes on a sandy or muddy hue due to the disturbance of the sea bed. By contrast, when looking out towards the horizon under a clear, cloudless sky, the sea sometimes seems to be a deep violet or blue-green, dark enough to be almost black, whilst under other conditions greys, greens, even pinks or pale violet can be seen. In practice, nearly all the colours you need can be found in the mixtures shown on page 28 or by adjusting them.

PAINTING THE SEA

Having composed your thoughts, you will, no doubt, be eager to make a colour sketch. This will be either in a form which might exist in its own right or as a reference for a more finished work to be made later at home.

In exposed places near the sea the conditions are often quite cool, damp or windy – sometimes all of these – so it is important to be suitably dressed and comfortable. A convenient boulder or rock slab can usually be found to sit on, so that your work can be placed on your lap with a water jar and other pieces of equipment to one side.

Most kinds of crayons or pastels can always be used but, in reasonable warmth and with a

▲ *This sketch was made as part of a study of the movement of the sea around rocks – a kind of 'snapshot' of one isolated part of the pattern of foam and water which came and went in a fraction of a second.*

▼ Surf
watercolour
12 × 40.5 cm (4¾ × 16 in)
The line of breakers made a focal point through the strong tonal contrasts of white foam, black rocks and the dark, inky blue of the sea. The running figures, foreground rock and its reflection gave other elements of interest. Such scenes are commonplace, but be alert to the possibilities they may offer.

little breeze to dry the paint, watercolour is an ideal medium. Consider acrylics also, since their quick-drying qualities can be a great advantage in other than very hot weather. Oil paints can be less convenient at the coast, normally requiring the use of an easel; neither is it always easy to handle wet canvases or boards when climbing the cliff path back to the car!

Do not lose sight of the decisions about your chosen composition which you made earlier. Then work boldly, aiming for the essence of the subject, especially the large main shapes, but ruthlessly disregard all irrelevant details. Remember that you will only have two or three hours in which to complete your work for, by that time, the light will have changed, possibly the weather also, and the tide risen or fallen perceptibly.

▶ Pulpit Rock
watercolour
33 × 16.5 cm (13 × 6½ in)
Sketched on the spot, the swirling water was carefully observed to identify specific patterns which repeated themselves. The tonal strength of each element was given special attention so as to produce the glistening texture of the sea and the contrast of the dark reflection from the rocks and cliff.

STUDLAND BAY

DEMONSTRATION IN WATERCOLOUR

The information for this painting came from a pencil sketch which included some written notes about the colours I saw and the effect of the late sun on a warm summer's afternoon. The method described is quite straightforward and consists of painting the lightest, biggest areas first, then laying increasingly stronger but smaller shapes until the final darkest accents fall into place. Each wash of colour was allowed to dry before another touched it.

COLOURS
Monestial Blue; French Ultramarine; Raw Sienna; Burnt Sienna; Cadmium Yellow; Crimson Alizarin.

FIRST STAGE
I started by photocopying the sketch (above) to the size I required and traced some of the main outlines on to 300gsm Waterford HP (very smooth) paper, which I had stretched to keep it taut and flat during working. Tracing the outlines ensures that no erasing will be required, with subsequent damage to the surface of the watercolour paper. With a little more confidence you can replace such pencil lines (which can be somewhat mechanical) with just a few guiding marks from a brush and some weak neutral colour (e.g. French Ultramarine and Burnt Sienna) to encourage a greater freedom of style.

With the top of my board *slightly* raised from the horizontal, I took a large and well-filled brush to lay very liquid washes of weak colours over each shape in turn – firstly, French Ultramarine graduated paler (with more water) as I painted downwards, adding a very little Crimson Alizarin near the horizon, then with varying mixtures of Monestial Blue and Raw Sienna or Cadmium Yellow for the sea and trees, followed by Burnt Sienna and Crimson Alizarin with a touch of French Ultramarine for the sandy beach. I also painted an almost imperceptible yellow with a tiny amount of the red to warm the white of the cliffs and boat. It is easy to make these first colours too strong and they were judged with considerable thought to ensure the right degree of contrast with the darker colours to follow. With watercolour it is especially important to plan each stage of the painting in advance, as it is difficult to make alterations later; aim to get the right tone and colour first time.

▲ *First stage*

SECOND STAGE
With all the white paper covered, darker strengths of similar colours were then laid, where appropriate, over the first pale tints, now dry. Some of these stronger colours were modified; for example, a little more blue was added in the shadow areas, a little yellow or red to warm the sunlit trees. All the while I sought to keep the work as broad as possible, avoiding unnecessary detail. The 'negative' shapes of the cliffs, boat and figures were achieved by painting the darker tones around them.

FINISHED STAGE
I now painted in the darkest tones, still making smaller shapes within shapes, finally placing the dark accents of the trees and reflections. Knowing when to stop is the last important decision to make and it is always better to lay down your brush sooner rather than later.

▲ *Second stage*

▼ *Finished stage*
Studland Bay, *watercolour*
24 × 34.5 cm (9½ × 13½ in)

SKIES AND ATMOSPHERE

Any skies which you include in your seascapes are of such great value that they deserve special attention and study. Often occupying a large proportion of the picture area, they can be used to give vivid impressions not only of space, open air and light, but also of coolness or warmth, dampness, mist and rain, sea breezes and strong winds, or just sunshine.

The patterns and colours of the sky are even more varied and quickly changing than those of the sea as clouds first develop, grow and then disperse in the movements of our weather systems. In turn, the mood of the sky and weather is reflected in the sea and shore below, which come under the influence of their sometimes unimaginable effects of light, shadows and colours.

▼ Skyscape
acrylic
25 × 29 cm (10 × 11½ in)
Big shapes give a strong visual impact, so when the sky is the main subject, it is often worth isolating one part of it and making it fill the picture.

◀ Winter Mooring
watercolour
20 × 20 cm (8 × 8 in)
When painting a sky out-of-doors, start by establishing one or two big shapes, in this case the blue at the top and, in weak colour, the large cloud below it, preserving any areas which are to be left as white paper. Other smaller shapes and darker colours can then be taken from similar clouds as they pass. Static parts, such as the boat and landscape, can be completed later, though it is still desirable to develop the painting as a whole if you can.

▼ Approaching Weather Front
watercolour
37 × 23 cm (14½ × 9 in)
Ragged cumulus clouds are forming and being pushed by a freshening wind under the high cirrus above, portending a change in the weather. The nearest grey cloud is darker, warmer in colour and appears larger than those further away, which tend to overlap and merge with each other. Such effects of perspective help to give a feeling of space and distance.

USE SKIES EFFECTIVELY

A seascape can be enhanced considerably and given its own special mood or atmosphere with an appropriate sky.

Build up your knowledge of cloud forms, colours and movements and the way they look by keeping a constant record of your observations, as always, in the form of sketches, drawings and notes. You will soon become aware of the ever-changing skies of great beauty and drama which are often to be seen.

CLOUD FORMATIONS

It will help your painting and enjoyment of skies if you can recognize some of the main cloud types and the kinds of weather associated with them.

Summarized briefly, they are:

- **Cirrus:** thin, white, wispy clouds, made of ice crystals and occurring at very high altitudes.
- **Cumulus:** heaps of lumpy or rounded clouds, sometimes with a flattened base and associated with warm summer afternoons.
- **Nimbus:** blankets of (usually) grey cloud, often giving rain.
- **Stratus:** broad layers of cloud of fairly uniform thickness like floating fog.

These classifications often merge into such combinations as **cirro-cumulus**, seen as patterns of very high, small, dappled clouds indicative of fine weather, or **cumulo-nimbus**, which are heaped clouds, often growing to great heights in rising warm air-currents to produce spectacular 'cauliflower' or 'anvil' shapes and frequently bringing thunder, heavy rain or hail.

◀ Carbis Bay
oil on canvas board
20 × 25 cm (8 × 10 in)
Compared with the cliffs and sea, the tonal range in the sky is quite small, therefore subtle contrasts of colour, especially of warmth and coolness, are necessary to provide variety and definition. For instance, the warmly tinted clouds at the top are of the same tone as the surrounding blue, but the difference in colour defines their shapes.

SKIES IN PERSPECTIVE

In drawing and painting skies, the effects of perspective again play an important role in creating a feeling of depth, space and recession. For instance, as cloud shapes retreat and converge into the distance, their relative sizes appear to diminish. At the same time, they lose their warmth of colour and appear even paler, more blue or grey.

Nearby overhead clouds are viewed more or less vertically, from below, and show us their darker, shadowed under-surfaces; but, unless silhouetted against the light, those which are further away reveal ever-increasing amounts of their sunlit sides and tops as we look at them more horizontally. Furthermore, when more closely packed, these distant clouds will overlap each other to provide yet another effect of perspective.

ATMOSPHERIC COLOURS

A cloudless sky is at its darkest and deepest blue directly overhead, becoming lighter and weaker in colour lower down until, seen through the haze just above the horizon, there is usually a warmth from tints of red, orange or yellow. However, skies are not often totally devoid of cloud, neither are they, when seen, the most interesting to the artist although they may give an instant impression of sunshine! Even apparently colourless 'white' or 'grey' clouds will provide some kind of interest in the form of tonal contrast and pattern. However, in practice, you will find it advantageous to look very hard to find *some* kind of colour in these so-called whites or greys to give them, at the very least, either a warmth or coolness; maybe an orange or pink tint in the whites, however weakly used, or some

MB = Monestial Blue
U = Ultramarine
CR = Cadmium Red
CA = Crimson Alizarin
CY = Cadmium Yellow

▲ *Crimson Alizarin, when mixed with the warmer Ultramarine, makes good violets and mauves, but, if the cooler Monestial Blue is substituted, the resulting colours are less pure though often appropriate for clouds and skies. It is impossible to make a good violet from Cadmium Red and Monestial Blue, though the subtle greys and browns which emerge are often very useful. A little yellow or Raw Sienna, if added to a red/blue mixture, will dull it towards grey.*

variations of violets or browns in the grey cloud shapes. Such colours do not have to be in any way strong or obvious, but they will add the contrasts of complementary colours in a very subtle way to what might otherwise be a sky with a dull monochromatic appearance.

Generally speaking, colours in the sky are at their most beautiful and spectacular when the sun is low, in winter for example, and particularly the periods just after sunrise or just before sunset. Any sketching that you can do then will be especially rewarding. At these times, however, you will not have long to work, so making colour sketches and notes might be the best approach. Then produce more careful paintings from these sketches as quickly as you can afterwards, whilst the vivid impressions are still clear in your mind.

Many of the colours you need can be derived from those shown in the charts on pages 28 and 48. Try varying the proportions and strengths of these mixtures to produce others, as well as experimenting with mixtures of your own choice.

SOME PRACTICAL PROBLEMS

Because most cloud patterns move and change comparatively quickly, a dry medium such as pastel or crayon might be a good choice as you will not then have to wait periodically for your work to dry. This problem may be a drawback when using watercolour, although it is a most effective medium in the right conditions. Acrylics are also recommended because they dry so readily and oil paints can be used even when it is raining!

Under rapidly changing conditions, use a bold approach to establish the big main shapes – there will be no time for small details. Your sky will quickly vanish, so put down the essentials at once. As with any other subject, try to make good decisions about composition, tone and colour, but, here, they will have to be made almost instantly! With these conditions and contrary to the usual advice, it is advantageous to work to quite a small size, about 20 x 25 cm (8 × 10 in) perhaps; this will avoid having to spend time mixing and applying large amounts of paint.

Painting skies can be a big challenge to even the most experienced. Mistakes are easily made but, as with anything else, practice and persistence will ensure the eventual delight of success, however modest.

▲ Fog, Portland Bill
watercolour
18 × 18 cm (7 × 7 in)
The sky is obscured by the fog, which works its own special kind of magic in creating a mysterious atmosphere. Colour and tonal contrasts rapidly diminish as objects recede into the all-enveloping greyness.

RAIN SQUALLS, GODREVY

DEMONSTRATION IN PASTEL

These low, scudding clouds raced along in the strong breeze, releasing their rain as they reached the shore. Because they moved and changed shape so quickly, I had to memorize my first vivid impressions of them as I drew in the main features. The information needed then, to build on and add to this basic idea, came from the similar, yet different patterns in the clouds which followed.

Pastels are a good medium for working quickly as there is no problem with drying.

COLOURS
Box of 36 assorted Rowney Artists' Soft Pastels, to which Warm Grey Tint 2, White (Cream Shade) and Prussian Blue Tint 1 were added.

FIRST STAGE
I started by taping a piece of Ingres blue-grey paper to a board and then lightly sketched the outlines and positions of the most important shapes with a dark grey pastel. I immediately fixed this with a light spray of 'Perfix' fixative from an aerosol (CFC free). Next, using the sides of pieces of pastel which I had broken off, I gently but freely rubbed on whites, blues, greys and greens to make a pale introduction to the composition. This allowed me to judge the way in which it would develop and I fixed the painting again, as I did at the end of each following stage.

▲ *First stage*

SECOND STAGE
Now I strengthened the darker tones of the clouds and landscape and intensified the whites and pale tints to increase the tonal contrasts, still mainly using the sides of the small pieces of pastels. The marks followed the forms of the clouds and rocks, but were otherwise made in vertical strokes. Many areas of the paper were deliberately left bare to allow its own colour to play a part in the picture.

I then paid more attention to the smaller shapes and colours of the rocky landscape and gave greater definition to the two figures in the foreground, using more variable marks.

▲ *Second stage*

▼ *Finished stage*
Rain Squalls, Godrevy
pastel
32 × 43 cm (12½ × 17 in)

FINISHED STAGE
Having established the painting to a substantial degree, I could now make some refinements and adjustments, especially by pressing the whites and light tints of the sky well into the paper's textured surface to build up solid, thick colour there; also by using the tips of the pastels to hatch oblique strokes over the greens, greys and buffs of the rocks and sand to create more exact colours and tones. In addition, oblique strokes of pale Prussian Blue were laid over the Cobalt Blue sky areas to make them cooler and lighter. When I drew the shadow on the lighthouse, I used the edge of a piece of thin paper as a mask to keep it well defined.

Finally, I lightly smudged the streaks representing the falling rain with my finger to give a soft effect here. Blurring pastel marks in this way should be done discretely as it can display a smooth, slick appearance if overdone. The remainder was left as it was drawn. A last light fixing completed the work.

BEACHES, ROCKS AND CLIFFS

It is at the shore where sea, sky and land all combine and fuse together to provide one all-embracing sensation. Here, we are in contact with the ground beneath us, whether of sand, pebbles, solid rock or grass, which we can touch or feel. We experience the smells of the sea, seaweed and mud, the feel of wind, rain or spray on our faces and the taste of salt on our lips. At the same time, we are conscious of space and distance, the brightness of light on the water and the colours and forms of beaches and rocks.

Seashores are never dull places! Standing there, one can always look out at wide vistas and distant views; yet, by a mere movement of one's head, the more immediate surroundings come into view, such as rocks, pools and the beach. Nearer still, there are sea-shells and pebbles, plants and creatures in and around the rock-pools, and small things washed up and exposed by the tides.

If there is a problem with painting on the seashore, it must surely be the overwhelming choice of subject.

▲ Rocky Beach
conté crayon
29.5 × 42 cm (11¾ × 16½ in)
This drawing is concerned with the markings on the rock surfaces and the way in which they lead the eye into the picture. The contrast shown between details of the immediate foreground and distant hill shapes across the bay gives a sense of depth and distance, whilst the two small figures give an added indication of scale.

COASTAL GEOLOGY

The main visual impact comes from the forms, colours and patterns of the geology which is characteristic of any particular part of the coast. They are dependent on the materials from which the rocks are made and in the way they are altered by the continuous action, over long periods of time, of the wind, rain, frost and the sea. In addition, man himself plays a part in the formation of the coast as a result of the structures he builds – quays, piers, groynes and breakwaters, for example – as well as by dredging and the removal of sands, shingle or rock.

A little knowledge of the materials and underlying geology which give the seashore its characteristic features not only adds to the interest of the subject but also to our understanding of what we see and why it appears as it does. It might be worth noting a few of the more common rock types and materials and how they affect coastal scenery visually:

- **Sands**, when damp, form wide level expanses, hard enough to walk on, yet soft enough to receive imprints. Dry sand is liable to be blown by the wind to form dunes which are sometimes held together by grasses. Depending on their source materials, colours can vary from white through greys, yellows and reds to dark browns.
- **Sandstones**, being soft, are prone to attack by both the sea and weather to form caves and narrow inlets. Interesting effects can often be seen in their wide variations of colour.
- **Limestone** and **chalk** are types of rock which are also attacked by the elements, the resulting erosion being apparent

▲ Stair Hole
watercolour
71 × 46 cm (28 × 18 in)
The low winter sunshine gives this strange geological structure a dramatic, theatrical effect. Always be ready to note any unusual conditions of light or weather which make your subject special.

◀ Brora, Sutherland
watercolour
22 × 33 cm (8½ × 13 in)
The river leads the eye through the sandy estuary into the middle distance where the white surf breaks on the pure blue sea. The dark cattle at the water's edge and the silhouetted houses give scale and a tonal reference point. Unless foreground detail is required, paint areas of grass or foliage as simple shapes of colour and tone rather than as a mass of individual leaves and stems.

in vertical cliff faces undermined by caves and inlets and fringed with reefs and stacks. Startling and dramatic effects are often produced by the brilliance of the white surfaces in sunshine.

- **Granites** are hard, crystalline, volcanic rocks that are much more resistant to erosion than the sandstones and limestones, but action by rain, frost and the sea over long periods of time eventually produces dramatic formations which resemble turrets, castles and masonry in many sombre but beautiful colours.

▲ Handfast Point
watercolour
33 × 48 cm (13 × 19 in)
This painting is composed of broadly rectangular and triangular shapes and is about the play of light and shade on the white chalk cliffs. Geometric shapes such as these often form a good structural basis for compositional ideas.

CHARACTER AND COLOUR

All these materials and geological structures create their own special characteristics; anyone looking at granite rocks will easily see how they differ from chalk cliffs or those of sandstone. Be observant of the intrinsic features which are special to each rock type and the way they help to make a location unique or to give it a particular 'feel'.

The various colours to be found in sands and rocks give another quality which merits attention and study. Dull greys of yellow, pink, red and violet seem to predominate but, even so, it is important to try to make them pleasing rather than to be satisfied with muddy, ambiguous colours. Judge them as carefully as you can, ensuring that you identify the underlying hue, which can then be given a little emphasis. Make full use, also, of any juxtaposed complementary colours, if you can find them, in order to add a little subtle vibrancy to what may otherwise be uninteresting groups of dull, nondescript greys. As if you did not have enough to think about, remember the importance of exact tonal relationships!

The greys and greens shown on page 28 can be taken as basic mixtures for those colours, but with some it is difficult to achieve the dull, dark greens of seaweed-covered boulders or the brown-greys of wet rocks. The chart opposite offers a few suggestions for mixing these but, again, it is worth experimenting with various proportions and strengths of these colours, together with any of your own discoveries, keeping notes of them for future reference.

FIGURES IN SEASCAPES

Many seashores, especially if they are inaccessible, are solitary places; at others, one often finds human activity to a greater or lesser degree. Unless your decision is to emphasize the loneliness of a place, consider the inclusion of at least one or two figures in your painting. They will add human interest, sometimes a vital spot of colour at a focal point or, most usefully, a sense of scale. By themselves, a group of rocks in a composition may seem unspectacular but, by introducing one or two people nearby, you can show them to be towering dramatically to a great height.

People on the beach create another kind of subject. When the opportunities occur, make a habit of drawing and sketching the little groups of figures there, either as compositional ideas in themselves or for later use in an otherwise empty seascape.

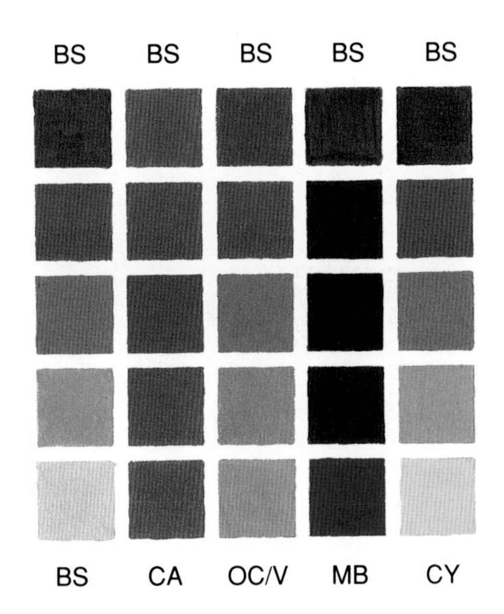

▲ *Burnt Sienna is an indispensable colour for beaches and rocks, either alone, as in the first column, or mixed with others. The beautiful dull green-greys of muddy sands and seaweeds at low tide are easily made from Burnt Sienna and Monestial Blue. If the orange-browns (right-hand column) are too bright, a tiny spot of Ultramarine will subdue them.*

BS = Burnt Sienna
CA = Crimson Alizarin
OC/V = Oxide of Chromium or Viridian
MB = Monestial Blue
CY = Cadmium Yellow

▼ Kimmeridge
watercolour
20 × 33 cm (8 × 13 in)
People have the habit of moving about! Try to fix the positions of some of them with simple shapes or outlines right at the start when sketching out-of-doors. Otherwise, it is likely that they may be overlooked until it is too late – either because no space is available or because everyone has gone home.

Where you work may depend to some extent on accessibility and sometimes you will have to choose between a very good position, although exposed and uncomfortable, or one which is less desirable but sheltered. The first option is likely to give the more exciting work, but it may have to be finished or repainted at home; in the other situation you may, at least, be able to paint or draw for a longer period and with greater concentration. Only you can decide at the time. Wind and cold are the main enemies and the only way to counter them is with adequate clothing, simple subjects and working methods, but, above all, a resolute mind.

What materials you take will depend on the conditions and how easy, or otherwise, it is to carry them. There are usually rocks or ledges to sit on, but a lightweight folding stool is useful on expanses of flat ground. Easels are seldom helpful in these often windy and rugged places.

Especially when conditions are difficult, be sure that you isolate just a small part of the scene and then make it fill the picture space; limit your composition to not more than a few bold, strong, contrasting shapes and discard all irrelevant details ruthlessly. There may well be little time for more than this, but if you do it well you will gain much satisfaction from the result.

▲ Helford Passage
pen and felt-tip markers
29.5 × 21 cm (11¾ × 8¼ in)
Markers dry instantly and different strengths of grey can be used to indicate tonal values. If you add pencilled colour notes, a lot of information can be contained within a small space.

SEASHORE DETAILS

Wandering, head down, along the tide-line of the shore, another world comes into focus to provide yet more ideas for the artist. Lying on or embedded in the wet sand are to be found pebbles and shells of all kinds and colours, pieces of wood bleached and smoothed into flowing shapes, chunks of cork, lengths of rope and old nets. Other, less pleasant, debris is also deposited there in the form of plastic objects, glass jars, bottles and crates from passing ships, dead sea-birds and strands of rotting seaweed.

Collect any such things, even if they seem unpromising subjects at the time. The very act of drawing or painting them will reveal features of unimagined and surprising interest. Studies of natural things are exceptionally rewarding, for example, the construction and design of spiral or other shells, a bird's plumage or skeleton, the jointed anatomy of crabs, comparisons of pebbles' textures and colours. Do not overlook the wind-blown plants which survive amongst the boulders above high-water level; but draw them where they grow, so that they remain undisturbed.

▲ Seashore Souvenirs
watercolour
19.5 × 23.5 cm (7¾ × 9¼ in)
Drawing and painting seemingly quite ordinary little objects found on the seashore, like these, will open your eyes to their remarkable diversities of form, colour and texture. Some of them can be intricate and a little challenging, so try just one or two simple examples at first. Especially if they are very small, paint them much larger – at perhaps three or four times their actual size.

THE TOMMY ROCK

DEMONSTRATION IN OIL

Although this is a simple composition, I spent some time thinking about how much to include, the proportions of light areas to dark areas, the placing of the focal point and the general mood of the subject. I then made two or three very small sketches, in pencil, which helped me with my decisions.

COLOURS
Titanium White; Monestial Blue; French Ultramarine; Raw Sienna; Burnt Sienna; Burnt Umber; Lemon Yellow; Cadmium Yellow; Viridian (hue); Cadmium Red (hue); Crimson Alizarin

FIRST STAGE
I selected a prepared canvas board to work on and started by sketching the outlines in charcoal. With a little Burnt Umber, well thinned with turpentine, I roughly scrubbed in the darkest shapes to help me to judge the strengths of the tones to come. The paint can be easily wiped off at this stage, but the turpentine will cause it to dry fairly quickly.

SECOND STAGE
When the first stage was dry, I painted in the shapes of the darkest shadows and reflections, my intention being to work from dark to light. For this purpose I mixed dark greens and violets, using the two blues, Siennas and Crimson Alizarin, thinned with turps. I delayed using any white

▲ *First stage*

▼ *Second stage*

paint for as long as possible, but, to develop the range of tones as work progressed, small amounts of it or Lemon Yellow were later included to lighten some colours. I now left the work to dry.

I mixed all the colours on my palette with a palette knife before picking up the paint with filbert-shaped brushes ('Bristlewhite' B12 Series in sizes from 1 to 6).

FINISHED STAGE

I began to develop the patterns of smaller shapes which describe the structure of the rock and its strata, for which I used the brushstrokes in definite and appropriate directions. Lighter, more opaque and thicker mixtures were needed now and I relied more on the viscosity of the paint itself, adding very little turps. I allowed the paint to dry once more before continuing.

The foreground water and sky had been neglected and it was time to develop those areas. They are the lightest parts of the picture and I wanted to keep the greatest tonal contrast against the dark vertical edge of the rock. The colours for the sea and sky contained quite a lot of white and were pale tints of the other colours in the composition. The work was completed by painting the bright light on the water with horizontal strokes of almost pure white paint applied thickly.

▲ *Finished stage*
The Tommy Rock
oil
25.5 × 30.5 cm (10 × 12 in)

BOATS AND HARBOURS

By their very nature, boats and harbours are functional structures where there is always activity and interest. Buildings around small fishing harbours are often quaintly old, made of local materials and tightly packed around the water's edge; along with them are well-worn slipways, quays, winches, derricks and cranes, posts and landing-stages. Larger modern harbours and ports, although arguably less romantic places, impress with their huge, geometrically formed and hard-edged equipment and buildings, such as overhead gantries, warehouses, liner-sized container ships and tankers.

The boats, large and small and for all sorts of purposes, come in a multitude of shapes and have many different methods of construction and propulsion. They are always surrounded by the paraphernalia of ropes, nets, ladders and lobster pots, booms, masts and sails, winches and oil drums, flags, buoys and bollards, in every conceivable colour from the dingiest to the brightest fluorescent.

DRAWINGS AND CREATIVITY

Images of boats and other marine objects can easily lapse into little more than technical illustrations, drawn with infinite care but devoid of emotional feeling. Even so, such drawings are often helpful as studies and a way of understanding the underlying structures of the things we see.

So rich and rewarding are the opportunities for creating compositions which are based on the patterns of shapes, textures and colours presented by boats and their surroundings that they seem to invite special attention. If you wish, the objects themselves could be simplified to such an extent that they almost lose their identity in the picture. They would be the starting point for your ideas and your chance to make something quite original from the things you have seen!

To try a composition like this, work at home from sketches. There, you will not be directly influenced by the subject, so giving full scope to your imagination and creativity.

▲ West Bay Harbour 1
watercolour
22 × 38 cm (8¾ × 15 in)
Avoiding any extreme effects of sunshine and shadows and ruthlessly disregarding all unnecessary detail will help to simplify a busy scene. The result may not be absolutely realistic – more a pattern of flat, decorative shapes, as in this example.

DRAWING BOATS

To many of us, boats have a great fascination, few seeming to be exactly alike and each having its own special characteristics. Whether seen lying on their sides in the mud of low tide or swinging around their moorings when afloat, careful observation will reveal their individual subtleties of design. For example, the curvature along the hull will depend on the purpose of the vessel – long and sleek in a fast power-boat, sharply curved around the broad beam of a rugged fishing-boat which works in rough seas. A boat viewed from an unusual angle when on dry land, below the stern for example, will show unexpected shapes and proportions to provide an exacting drawing exercise. Nothing can be taken for granted!

LIGHT ADDS INTEREST

Sometimes the expected colours are missing from the harbour – the sky is probably overcast, everywhere a uniform greyness. But imagine the transformation when a low, late evening sun gives warmth, the interest of long shadows and an almost theatrical effect. See how a strong overhead sun will break up a grey dullness into strong patterns of deep shadows and intensely bright surfaces. Consider, as well, the often overlooked effects of an *absence* of light! The mysterious cool light of the moon perhaps? Even total darkness apart from any illumination provided by artificial light? Introduce a little mist or fog and you will have created a really spooky atmosphere.

Using the effects of light is a good way to add interest to greyness in a scene, but remember that greys can be given interest, also, if they are enriched with the subtle contrasts of complementary colours or warm and cool tints.

▲ Night Mooring
watercolour
30.5 × 23 cm (12 × 9 in)
The fishing boat and dinghy gain an added element of interest through being silhouetted against the low sun; the focus of the picture thus changes from the boats themselves to the effect of light on and around them.

EMERALD ISLE

DEMONSTRATION IN ACRYLIC

Acrylic paints are diluted with water or an acrylic medium, but become waterproof when dry and can be overpainted endlessly. It is possible to apply them in a succession of thin, transparent layers known as 'glazes', in thicker, opaque colours or as a combination of both, to allow easy and adaptable methods of working.

My interest was in the surface patterns and solid bulk of this boat undergoing repairs.

COLOURS
Lemon Yellow; Cadmium Yellow; Raw Sienna; Burnt Sienna; Cadmium Red; Crimson Alizarin; Ultramarine; Monestial Blue; Oxide of Chromium.

▲ *First stage*

FIRST STAGE
I worked on 'Not' surface watercolour paper, which I stretched because I like to paint on a taut surface. Alternatively, I could have used card, canvas, wood or hardboard, prepared with three or four coats of acrylic 'gesso' primer to give a pleasing white surface.

Pencil outlines were lightly drawn, then, using a 19mm (¾ in) Cryla flat brush (Series C15), I washed Burnt Sienna diluted with water and a few drops of acrylic medium over much of the boat and foreground areas. In a similar way, diluted Ultramarine covered parts of the sky, the shadow side of the cabin and the far end of the boat.

SECOND STAGE
I now began to paint other colours over the first basic compositional shapes, working first in one part of the picture, then in another, trying all the time to build it up as a whole. However, perhaps I spent more time than I should in dealing with the warm colours at the bottom of the hull and the supporting props – but I was anxious to clarify the detail in these areas.

Most of these warm colours were painted on as glazes, one over another. Although the paint was quite liquid, I was able to work continuously, without needing at any time to wait for the surface to dry.

▲ *Second stage*

FINISHED STAGE
I now strengthened the colours around the rudder, stern and rusty oil-drum and painted the intense green patches on the side of the boat. For this I used the opaque Oxide of Chromium, which I modified in places with yellow, the Siennas, blue or white to provide variations. With acrylics it is easy to paint one colour over another, the effects obtained depending on the transparency, or otherwise, of the colours used.

Finally, I added a few details with a small, round Cryla brush (Series C10) and a long-haired 'rigger' for the ropes.

▼ *Finished stage*
Emerald Isle
acrylic
37 × 45 cm (14½ × 17¾ in)

CONCLUSION

◄ West Bay Harbour 2
acrylic
42.5 × 42.5 cm (16¾ × 16¾ in)

You will have realized, by now, that in drawing and painting seascapes there are many aspects to consider and I hope that this book will be helpful in explaining some of them, however briefly. The important thing, now, is to get started.

It will be necessary to do a lot of work out-of-doors, looking keenly, analysing what you see and gathering information in the form of drawings and sketches. Balance this with work at home, where you will have time to consider the evidence of your sketchbooks and to use your imagination. Although drawing is important, do not let it interfere with your painting; the one will help the other and each will improve, however slowly and gradually, with practice. At first, do not be too ambitious and choose simple, bold subjects without too much detail.

Two practical obstacles to overcome may be not only in setting aside enough time for painting, but also in finding a suitable place to work at home. Having to pack and unpack your materials and work each time can be a serious deterrent. The ideal solution is to have your own work room (it can be quite small) but, where this is not possible, try to preserve some little corner where your work can be left out. If you can only go to your painting and pick up a waiting brush, you will find that you have been working all morning or evening without realizing it!

I am quite sure you will discover that painting seascapes will be a totally absorbing and satisfying interest.